SOUTHAMPTON'S OLD KINGSLAND
AND ST MARY STREET

SOUTHAMPTON'S
OLD KINGSLAND
AND ST MARY STREET

DAVE MARDEN

First Published in Great Britain in 2020 by DB Publishing,
an imprint of JMD Media Ltd

ISBN 9781780916132

Printed and bound in the UK

CONTENTS

ACKNOWLEDGEMENTS

D uring the writing of this book it has been my pleasure to compile records of the long lost streets of Kingsland, together with a glimpse back at St Mary Street as it used to be in its thriving heyday. I am most grateful to those who have contacted me with photos and memories of the past and, as ever, my sincere thanks to the staff at Southampton City Archives for their help and permission to use so many of the precious images held in their records, without which this book would not have been possible. Other images have arrived from various sources and, despite my best efforts, it has not been possible to trace the origin of some. If I have inadvertently infringed anyone's copyright or ownership, I sincerely apologise.

INTRODUCTION

The neighbourhoods of Kingsland and St Mary's have been linked together throughout Southampton's history, with St Mary Street forming the eastern boundary of Kingsland, the other borders being North Front, West Front (now part of Palmerston Road) and South Front.

The area of St Mary's dates back to Saxon times and the old settlement of Hamwic, which was also a principal south-coast port. Its main thoroughfare, once known as Love Lane, ran northwards from East Street towards what is now the Avenue and, at its southern end, St Mary's Church was founded in the eighth century.

As the name suggests, Kingsland was once owned by a monarch, in this instance King Richard I, and the land was later passed on to St Denys Priory, but by the 13th century it had been purchased by the town. It is thought that orchards once covered the area in medieval times, but many of the early buildings were established in the 1820s and the following decades of industrialisation saw the locale filled with working-class housing for the sprawling population.

In the Victorian era, such accommodation was, at best, very poor and often pitiful. As Southampton moved into industrial times, workmen and their families arrived from the surrounding rural districts to find little or no accommodation available, so overcrowding became commonplace. To meet this demand, streets of poor-quality housing were literally thrown up by landlords eager to cash in on the population explosion. In many cases the buildings themselves were poorly constructed, without damp courses and with the upper floors merely composed of lath and plaster covered in wooden boards or slates to fend off the elements. Often these would be built back to back with no through ventilation, resulting in damp and stuffy conditions, made all the worse with whole families being packed into a single room.

As the situation worsened, more groups of houses were squeezed into small plots between existing buildings, forming dingy courts entered by narrow alleyways. Such places were often set under the shadow of tall surrounding tenements, hardly ever seeing sunlight and, under such conditions of damp and decay, illness was commonplace.

To add to this misery, water was supplied from a single tap in the courtyard where there was usually a common privy over an ash pit.

As the 20th century approached, a document on slum dwellings was published in 1893, titled the *Dilapidated & Unhealthy Houses Report*, detailing the parlous state of working-class housing with many properties being condemned, or beyond habitation, while others were literally falling down. The nooks and crannies of the town were detailed street by street. Worst of all were the ancient buildings in the old town and those in Holy Rood, but the courts in Kingsland were not far behind and also came in for special criticism.

In the 18th and 19th centuries, the habitations of poor and undesirable people living in crowded tenements were the sort of areas no outsider would dare to enter – unless by invitation from one of the local 'ladies', or under escort from the local policeman in pursuit of a felon. Some of the dwellings in Kingsland during the darkest Victorian period of the mid- and late-1800s would have been foreboding. That said, many of the houses lining the main streets were of an acceptable standard (for the time) and offered decent homes for people to live in.

However, many of those streets dated back to the 1820s, being poorly constructed with little sanitation and running water. By the turn of the 20th century, these crumbling buildings were well overdue for demolition. As it was, most lingered on until clearance orders came in the 1930s.

By then, most people living there were making the best of their lives in their woefully inadequate homes, but even so were reluctant to leave the neighbourhoods they had grown up in. By the outbreak of the Second World War most of the streets had been cleared and it was not until peacetime returned that the district was resurrected with decent homes with modern (for then) facilities.

Most Sotonians will have visited St Mary Street at some time in their lives, but the street itself has undergone considerable changes over many generations. Consisting almost entirely of shops and pubs, it was the hub of activity for those living in the area. Many of its old buildings have been cleared away and replaced by modern counterparts, but a few of its original structures remain, albeit almost unrecognisable now with modern frontages. In its entirety it ran from East Street at its southern end up to Northam Road at Six Dials in the north.

St Mary Street had remained a semi-rural byway until the 1820s when the town began to grow and became more industrialised. The mid-1800s saw the arrival of the railway and the building of the docks and, from that time, the St Mary's area became densely populated with streets of terraces to house the ever-growing workforce that served those industries. In the midst of it all, St Mary Street became the local centre for shops, services, pubs, worship and entertainment.

From the latter 19th century until the Second World War, the street was a magnet for shoppers and its busy market place on Kingsland Square offered bargains that drew locals and other townsfolk to its bustling pavements. The many pubs and dining rooms also flourished, while entertainment was available from the local musical hall and cinema. Late-night shopping was also to be had from the many stores and stalls decked out with strings of lanterns trading well into the night. The coming of the electric tram in 1901 saw a boost in trade as several routes ran through the street bringing more people in from the suburbs.

After substantial damage to the area by wartime bombing, the street never really recovered and, during the 1950s, became a shadow of its former magnificence with many buildings, by then 100 years old or more, beginning to show their age and falling into disrepair, with many of the surrounding streets being demolished and most of the local inhabitants being scattered to other parts of the town. Some returned when the modern housing estate was built on Golden Grove in the 1960s and 1970s but, for the most part, many of those in their new homes knew little of old streets and what had been there before.

The building of the dual-carriage road named Kingsway in the 1960s served only to isolate St Mary Street and the steady decline was accelerated. This being despite several improvement schemes that failed to revive both the street and its market.

Through the pages of this book we shall take an imaginary stroll through the streets of Kingsland and St Mary Street itself, visiting homes, shops, pubs and businesses to see who the occupants were from back in the 1830s until the 1960s, after which so many changes took place.

For the most part, the maps used in this book are based on those of the Ordnance Survey in 1910, which represent the area at the height of its past, while some others show the later layout of buildings that have changed since then. As ever, in the old streets there have been many changes over the generations, particularly in the numbering systems that differed so much as the streets grew and the various groups of buildings were slowly absorbed into it. I have done my very best to link these to their modern-day addresses but the old directories often show several numbers duplicated – or sometimes no numbers at all. With the standard of education being variable in those days, there were several errors just to complicate matters for the later historians! To save much confusion, all premises are referred to by their latter-day numbers.

Dave Marden, 2020

A pre-World War Two aerial picture of the Kingsland area as it was before redevelopment, with St Mary Street running left to right across the bottom third of the photograph.

PART ONE – KINGSLAND

NORTH FRONT

North Front was by far the longest of the Kingsland streets, running westwards from the top of St Mary Street, before turning south-west to meet West Front (now Palmerston Road). Much of the street ran alongside the main Southampton to London railway line.

In the early years the street was divided into three sections, with West Front to Cossack Street being North Front Upper, then Cossack Street to Cross Street being North Front Middle, and the remainder to St Mary Street known as Kingsland Place Each part had its own numbering system, all of them beginning at No. 1. The latter day numbering system dates from around 1870 with Nos. 1 to 51 running along the south side from St Mary Street to Palmerston Road, then back on the north side with Nos. 52 to 74 and this is the numbering I have used to avoid confusion.

The streets of Kingsland in the early 1900s, bounded by North Front, West Front, South Front and St Mary Street.

The south side of North Front from St Mary Street showing Nos. 1 to 14 and the Holy Trinity Church.

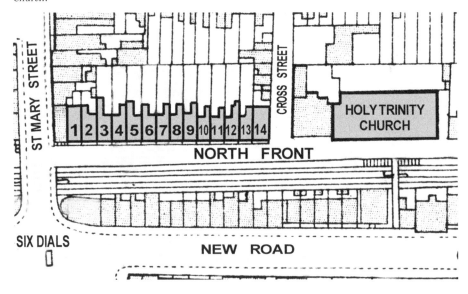

NORTH FRONT – SOUTH SIDE NOS. 1 TO 14

In the directories of the 1840s this section of the street was called Eastern Place or Kingsland Place and was home to mainly skilled workers. Henry Burgess was at No. 1 and earned his living as a letter carrier or postman from 1843 to 1851, as did John Burgess snr, his son further along the street at No. 10.

No. 2 was the home of brush maker Robert Berry from 1839 but by the 1840s he had changed his skills to basket making. Railway gatekeeper William Aldridge followed him in the 1850s. Master mariner C. F. Starke and his family were at No. 3 from 1845 until the late 1880s, but during that time their name had mysteriously changed to Sparks! Shipwright James Lock was at No. 4 in the 1840s, followed by the seafaring Newell family in the 1860s.

Coal carrier W. Watson was one of the early names listed at No. 5 in the 1830s, and there followed an assortment of slaters, plasterers, a shoe maker, whitesmith and a warehouseman. Next door at No. 6, stonemason John Weeks eked a living through the 1840s followed there by seaman George Frampton and dressmaker Elizabeth May through the 1860s and 1870s, while No. 7 saw the likes of schoolmaster Richard Kennett and railway policeman Francis Spencer in the 1830s and 1840s. Water inspector Stephen Mansbridge appeared through the 1860s.

In the 1830s No. 8 saw blacksmith Jeremiah Forest as one of its earliest householders. He was followed by tailoress Sarah Fling, before engine driver Henry Wallbridge saw out the 1860s there. Then the 1870s saw a health inspector with the unfortunate name of Thomas Hazard, prior to a brick layer, the usual boot maker, and ships storekeeper Thomas Flew, all before the turn of the century. The occupants of No. 9 were unremarkable apart from the Hartup family who lived there from the early 1900s through to the very end.

Letter carrier John Burgess, son of Henry at No. 1, lived at No. 10 back in the 1830s. The 1840s and 1850s saw a number of ladies at that address, including Mrs Newman, widow Mrs Mary Carter and laundress Mary Sharman. Painter John Patton (or Payton) was there in the 1870s ahead of a slater, a carter and a ships stoker before Frederick Fryer became its longest resident from around 1912 through to the street's demolition. No. 11 housed blacksmith Josiah Smith back in 1851, and shoe maker John Smith was there from 1861 until the mid-1880s.

A view of North Front from the top of St Mary Street in 193,3 looking west towards the Holy Trinity Church on the left. The main railway line to London runs behind the long wall, which is topped with hazardous spikes. The buildings on the right are along New Road and the footbridge over the railway in the middle distance linked New Road with the church. There were three such pedestrian bridges linking Kingsland with New Road.

The early buildings that were known as Kingsland Place, looking east towards the top of St Mary Street near the railway bridge.

The wartime ruins of the Holy Trinity Church pictured in 1941, soon only the tower and spire would remain.

The Holy Trinity Church had stood in North Front since 1827. It was originally built as a chapel for the adjoining women's prison (see Cross Street) and was enlarged in 1847 to accommodate the growing local population. Almost a century later it was badly damaged by wartime bombing raids and mostly demolished. By 1944 only the spire remained, in an unsafe condition, and this was finally knocked down in 1950.

NORTH FRONT – SOUTH SIDE NOS. 15 TO 27

Nos. 15 to 27 North Front were referred to as Middle North Front in the early directories and originally had a separate numbering system from either end of the street. No. 15

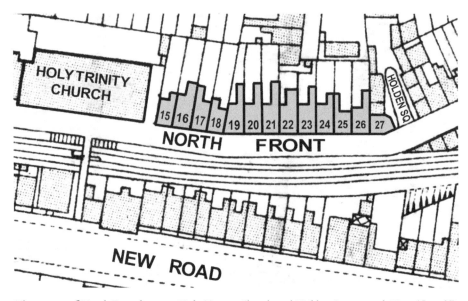

The section of North Front between Holy Trinity Church and Holden Square with Nos. 15 to 27.

was the abode of several boot and shoe makers, with Edward Hellyar residing there from 1847 until 1851, after which Richard Harraway took up the trade from 1871 until 1887. George Curtis was the final inhabitant there, having moved in in around 1912.

In its time, No. 16 was home to builder Thomas A. Gates, laundress Mary Crocker, and blacksmith Edwin Cane, long before the Sparkmans were there from 1907 until about 1925, while a Mrs Pearce was the last tenant. Next door, at No. 17, Frederick Axford was another long-term resident from 1912 until the end. Dock porter Albert George Lawrence was at No. 18 from 1901 until 1920. Way back in 1836 cabinet maker George Ockleford lived at No. 19 and remained there for 30 years, with Edward George Mansbridge there for the final two decades from 1916.

Gas inspector James Godden appears at No. 20 in 1884 and the same name is registered there through to the street's final days. Carpenter Thomas Petty and his wife were in No. 21 through the 1840s and 1850s, other later residents being basket maker John Doling, journeyman tailor William Watts, 'mangler' Mrs Sara Smith and marine-store dealer William Harman, with George Henry Cavell being the final householder there from around 1920. No. 22 was the home of coach smith George Payne from 1847 until 1861 and cow keeper James Hillier was at No. 23 in the 1840s, with letter carrier John Godley moving in after him and remaining there until 1851.

North Front from No. 19 looking east to No. 15 with the Holy Trinity Church towering above.

The Burgess family were the early residents at No. 24 from the 1840s until the 1860s, with John Jnr being a letter carrier (see also Henry Burgess at No. 1 and J. Burgess Snr at No. 10) and his daughter Jane Maria working as a milliner and dressmaker. No. 25

Looking back from No. 27 to No. 19 North Front towards St Mary Street with the spire of the Holy Trinity Church in the distance.

saw the Stride family living there from 1901 until Thomas William Stride was the last at that address. Pedlar Joseph Gilbertie was the earliest occupant of No. 26, later followed by laundress Eliza Scullard in 1851. Later tenants were blacksmith James Shotter, whitesmith Charles Taylor, bricklayer George Henry Blake and decorator Frederick Dawkins, with Cyril George Glover being the final name in the rent book from 1925. The usual smattering of working-class tenants occupied No. 27 on the corner of Holden Square

NORTH FRONT – SOUTH SIDE NOS. 28 TO 40

Cabinet maker John Hillyer Snr lived at No. 28 from 1843 and his son, also John, a cabinet maker, lived next door at No. 29 in 1851. Nickholes Squires was a later tenant there at No. 28 before and during World War One but there were no other long-term occupants. Walter Whitlock was the only long term householder at No. 29 from 1916 until 1931. Between Nos. 29 and 30 was the passageway to Isaac's Court (see later in this chapter). No. 30 saw several long-stay tenants with gentleman William Green there from 1836 until 1849, followed by police sergeant Charles Clift (previously at No. 31) who stayed until 1863, and finally the Marshman family from 1901 until the end.

Nos. 28 to 40 on the south side of North Front, either side of Cossack Street. No. 34 on the corner was the Royal Oak pub.

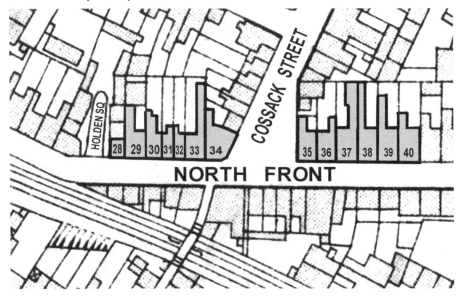

Mrs Harriet Rose lived at No. 31 from 1851 and made a living selling eggs until 1876. John Page was at that address from 1907 until demolition came. Carpenter Aaron Lanham was the key holder to No. 32 in the 1840s and the Cluetts were the final tenants there from 1914. No. 33 was another of those households that seemed to keep their occupants longer than most. Carpenter Lewis Lane was first in from the 1840s until at least 1876. Laundress Jane Ward was another who felt no need to wander, being there from 1901 until 1925.

No. 34 was the *Royal Oak* pub, where William Draper was an early beer seller. Charles Lane was the first recorded landlord under the pub's name in 1851, remaining behind the bar until Charles Knowlton presided from the 1880s when the premises belonged to the Winchester Brewery. He was succeeded by James Payne until Harry J. Earle took over in 1912. The final bartender was Frederick Sparkes, who was in charge when the pub was refused a licence and closed in 1926. It then became a fish and chip shop run by James Burt.

On the corner opposite the *Royal Oak* was a shop at No. 35, once the premises of egg merchant George Rose back in the 1870s (see Harriet Rose at No. 31). A decade later, wardrobe dealer Mrs J. Veal was there but by 1901 horse keeper and groom William Cox had made it into a general shop in which he and his wife Mary Ann served until the final days of the street when daughter Elsie had taken over. Wardrobe dealers appear fairly frequently – the term actually applies to buyers and sellers of second-hand clothes!

Boot maker David Annett and his family were at No. 36 from 1901 until the end and James Miller next door at 37 was there almost as long, having moved in around 1912. Bricklayer Jacob Laver occupied No. 38 from 1839. He was followed by blacksmith Sam Thresher into the 1850s. Afterwards came the Thomas family from 1914, and finally Frank Edmonds saw out the remaining decade. Coach smith James Wilson had a long association with No. 39, living there from 1843 until 1871, with Frederick Arthur Mayhew covering a similar length of period from 1912 onwards.

Shoe maker George Rodwell plied his trade at No. 40 back in the early 1860s until the late 1880s, while Henry England and his family were final tenants at that address, having been there since 1907. The Tuck family appears at No. 41 in 1871 with coach painter Edmund and brush maker Henry Thomas spanning the decades until 1931.

Letter carrier John Burgess Snr had previously occupied No. 10 back in the 1830s, but by 1843 he was living at No. 42 where he ran a pub called the *Flying Postman*, but the venture appears to have been short lived and he carried on with his postal duties there until 1876. Brush maker John Healy lived there from 1912 until the business was carried on by James Brett in 1920. He and his wife stayed until the street was cleared.

Thomas Bickers was a carver and gilder living at No. 43 back in 1836 until 1850 when Mrs Sarah Marshall took over the tenancy. She was there until the 1860s. The Downings were there in the 1870s until Francis Dominy had set up a general shop there by 1884 but that was gone by the time the Cluett family saw out the remaining years from 1907.

'Proprietor of House' was the title of widower James Prior, who lived in No. 44 from 1839 until 1853, possibly one of the few owner occupiers. Master wheeler George Blackman was there in the 1870s and William Price from 1912 until the 1930s.

NORTH FRONT – SOUTH SIDE NOS. 41 TO 51

The western end of North Front showing Nos. 41 to 50. No. 51 is the Angel Inn which became No. 22 Palmerston Road.

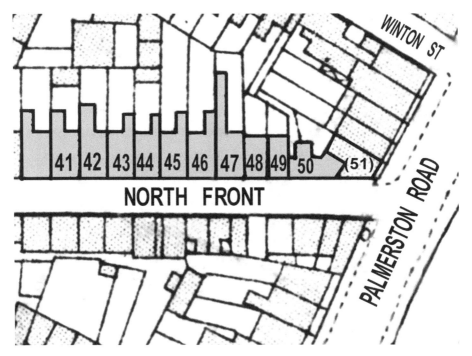

Nos. 47 to 34 North Front looking eastwards. On the distant corner is No. 34 which was the Royal Oak pub.

HOLDEN SQUARE

Holden Square, also known as Holden's Court or Holden's Place, appears in the 1851 census, where six tenants are named, three of them being women laundresses, one of whom was Sarah Webb, who was still there a decade later. The 1884 directory lists eight houses – six of them being inhabited by labourers.

At first glance, the houses in Holden Square seem a pleasant enough oasis with gardens and a gated entrance set back between Nos. 27 and 28 off the south side of North Front, but, in reality, they were not exactly idyllic. In fact, the condition of the houses was roundly condemned in the 1893 slum report, five being back to back with other buildings allowing no through-ventilation.

Originally, a ninth house stood in the middle of the square, which was singled out as being unfit for habitation and was closed by order of the magistrates due to its unhealthy state and the smallness of its rooms. It was also noted to be an unhealthy influence on the adjacent No. 3 and demolition was recommended. It would appear that Nos. 4 and

5 were built from wood and hung with slates, while the 1901 census notes No. 6 had been pulled down. At the time of the report, the water supply and sanitary convenience was located in the courtyard but with no ash pit available.

Laundress Ann McKay was an early resident at No. 1 in the 1850s, succeeded by a number of labourers intil the Wilson family moved in around 1920. Another laundress, Sarah Webb, was at No. 2 in the early days followed by the usual succession of labourers, while No. 3 housed yet another laundress, this time Joanne Soper, in the 1851 census. Arthur James Bull was later a long time tenant there from the early 1900s until the 1930s.

No. 4 was home to seaman George H. Penny and nurse Eliza Privet before Mrs Cameron arrived in 1914 and saw out the final years there. No. 5 gave shelter to many labourers in its time while No. 6 had been pulled down following the 1893 report.

Mary Ball at No. 7 was yet another laundress who inhabited the square in its early days and, finally, No. 8 saw several seamen, a sawyer and a dock labourer beneath its roof over time.

No. 27 North Front on the left, with Nos. 1 to 3 Holden Square.

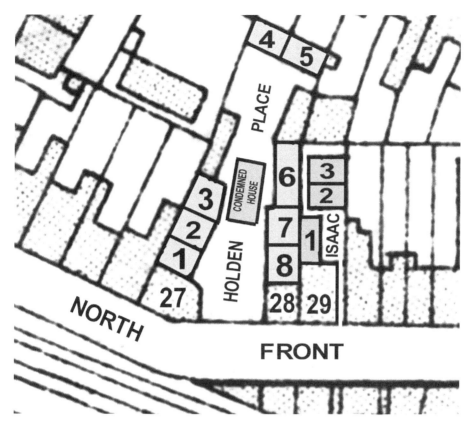

The poor original buildings that formed Holden Place showing Nos. 1 to 8, with the condemned house in the centre, also showing the adjacent Isaac's Court where Nos. 1 to 3 were also in a grim setting.

NORTH FRONT – SOUTH SIDE – HOLDEN SQUARE NOS. 1 TO 8

Nos. 2 to 8 Holden Square with Nos. 4 and 5 in the distance.

ISAAC'S COURT

NORTH FRONT – SOUTH SIDE – ISAAC'S COURT NOS. 1 TO 3

The three houses of Isaac's Court were accessed via a narrow passage through No. 29 North Front with No. 1 being back to back with those in Holden Place and all three being deprived of light and air. They were described as damp, dark and unhealthy. The third house had been unoccupied in 1871 and dilapidated by 1893. There seems to be very little documentation of those living there and, as with neighbouring Holden Place, the toilet and water supply was located out in the court with no ash pit.

NORTH FRONT – NORTH SIDE NOS. 52 TO 62

This section of North Front ran east from Palmerston Road. George Cooper was resident at No. 52 from the First World War until the final days and the Puckett family was nearby at No. 54 for a similar period. There was then a gap in the buildings before

The north side of North Front from 52 to 63A, where Nos. 61 and 62 were once a pub named the Trinity Arms. North Cottage and Stanley Cottage stood next door. A passageway between Nos. 57 and 58 led through to Exmouth Place.

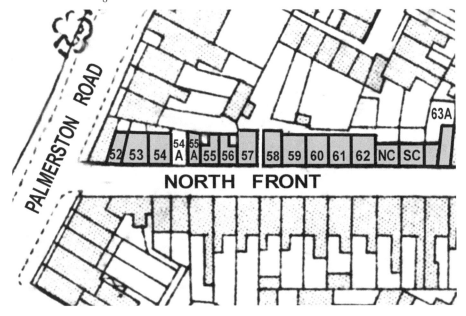

On the right stand Nos. 52 to 62 North Front with Nos. 23 to 24 Palmerston Road nearest the two ladies.

Nos. 67 to 52 North Front with the protruding entrance to No. 63 that was once the coach building premises of Henry Riggs.

reaching No. 55A, which was sometimes called 54A in the old directories. In the latter years this was occupied by confectioner Alice Keene and then finally by wireless dealer Henry Nunn. The Oddy family were at No. 57 for the final two decades, next door to the cut way that led through to Exmouth Place. This had once been the home of coach wheeler John Dean in the 1860s. No. 58 was inhabited by Walter Newman, who saw out the street's final years there from World War One.

Nos. 61 and 62 were once the *Trinity Arms* (later the *Trinity Inn*), which dated back to 1871 when John Kedgley was selling beer there. Owned by Mew Langton's Newport Brewery, it was refused a licence in 1909 and converted to two residences. No. 61 was then occupied by tailoress Mrs Jessy Gledhill through to the 1920s, while No. 62 became the home of William Blundell from World War One until the street's final years.

Next to the pub were two cottages named North Cottage and Stanley Cottage, which appeared in the early 1900s. The Rolls family were in North Cottage for almost all its existence, while Edward John Mansbridge was an early resident of Stanley Cottage.

NORTH FRONT – NORTH SIDE NOS. 63A TO 74

The last line of North Front buildings were opposite the end of Cossack Street. These were Nos. 63 to 74. No. 63A was a yard that was once the premises of coal dealer William Cox for about 20 years after the turn of the century.

The yard may once have belonged to coach builder Henry Riggs, who had set up as a blacksmith at No. 63 back in the early 1840s and then became a coach maker, a trade he mastered until the late 1880s. In the mid-1840s there were no less than a dozen inhabitants of North Front that were involved in the coach-building business either as builders, wheelwrights or painters. After the demise of coach building, Charles Barnes had moved into No. 63 and remained there until the street was cleared.

No. 64 was once a shop, mainly a greengrocer's, from way back in the 1850s when John Kinchington ran it through to the late 1880s, but Henry Hoare appears to have been the last shopkeeper there in the early 1900s. No. 68 was also a shop, being a grocer's from the time of William Henry Matthews in the 1880s. George Frederick Isles had taken over from around 1912 and stayed on until the very end. Between Nos. 68 and 69 was a passage leading to Waterloo Bridge (which see).

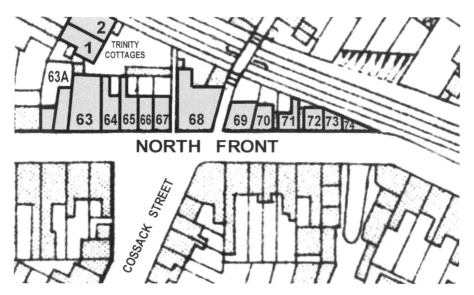

NORTH FRONT

The final section of North Front from Nos. 63A to 74 that were opposite the north end of Cossack Street where No. 63 had long been the premises of coach builder Henry Riggs. The cut way between Nos. 67 and 68 led to the two Trinity Cottages.

Nos. 69 to 71 North Front showing Waterloo Passage, the cut way on the left, which was a footway over the railway to New Road. In this 1935 photograph Nos. 72 to 74 had been demolished.

Nos. 71 to 74 North Front marked the end of the houses on the north side of the street where it met the wall that ran alongside the main railway line to London.

Nos. 69 to 74 were tucked into a small triangle of land alongside the railway. The Standbrook (or Stanbrook) family were in No. 70 from the time of World War One until the buildings came down, while next door, at No. 71, Charles Spencer was there for even longer, having moved in during the early 1900s. The final three houses were very small and appear to have been demolished in the early 1930s, before the rest the street came down. Mrs Northover was at No. 73 from before the First World War.

EXMOUTH PLACE

The 1893 slum report published details of the appalling living conditions in the various Victorian courts, as well as other places that were tucked away from the main streets. Exmouth Place was of the more fortunate examples that, although omitted from the report, must still have been an unpleasant place to live.

Exmouth Place was a continuation of Exmouth Street, which ran off the south side of New Road and the cluster of 12 houses were accessed via a footbridge over the

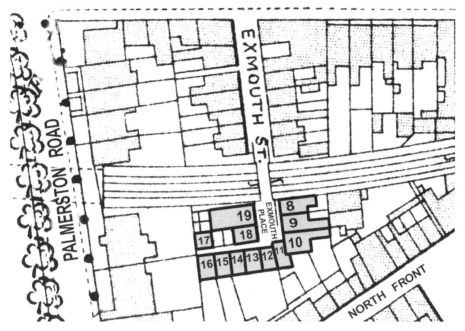

The cluster of houses that were Exmouth Place, reached by a footbridge over the railway.

This photo shows the approach and footbridge from Exmouth Street with Nos. 11 and 12 Exmouth Place.

Nos. 13 to 16 Exmouth Place were tucked in a narrow passage leading off the main court.

main railway line, as well as from North Front. Apart from the six homes immediately near the footbridge, the others lined a tiny courtyard that was not more than a narrow passage. It must have been extremely claustrophobic living there.

There was obviously a strong neighbourly spirit in those homes as many residents lived together for many years. The Dennys at No. 8 were previously in No. 10 before the

Pearce family moved in during the First World War. The Anteneys at No. 11, the Locks at No. 12 and the Whites at No. 13 were all together from the early 1900s, as were the (other) Locks at No. 15 and the Foremans at No. 16.

The dead end of the narrow passage at Exmouth Place with No. 16 on the left and No. 17 on the right.

TRINITY COTTAGES

Between Nos. 67 and 68 North Front ran a passage through to the two Trinity Cottages at the rear of the buildings. Not many details are included in the directories but No. 1 had been the home of carriage painter George Bishop back in the 1870s. The Short family had taken over that address from the early 1900s until the late 1920s. No. 2 was the home of carpenter Anthony Westbury in the 1870s and house decorator James Terrell had moved in from around the turn of the century and was there to around 1912. Tom Barnes and Joseph Saunders were its later tenants.

WATERLOO BRIDGE

Between Nos. 68 and 69 North Front was Waterloo Bridge, otherwise known as Waterloo Passage, which was a cut way to New Road which led over a footbridge crossing the main railway line to London. On the north side of the bridge was a small group of cottages – aptly named Waterloo Bridge. There were five in all – Nos. 1 to 4 and another named Waterloo Cottage. There seems to be no mention of these before the 1901 census. Perhaps being tucked away they escaped the attention of officials, but that early entry lists dock labourer William Watkins in Waterloo Cottage, flower seller Emily

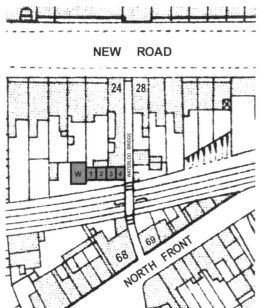

Northover at No. 1, Eliza Manton at No. 2, mariner George Fulton at No. 3 and coal porter Frank Watkins at No. 4. Seaman Patrick Long moved into No. 1 before World War One and stayed until the late 1920s. Laundress Annie Montague (No. 2) and carter George Blake (No. 3) arrived at about the same time and both stayed until the area was cleared in the 1930s.

The small group of cottages at Waterloo Bridge, accessed via a passage that ran from North Front to New Road.

Waterloo Cottage on the left with others that made up the small group at Waterloo Bridge, as seen from the railway bridge.

CRAVEN STREET

Craven Street ran west from St Mary Street to Cossack Street. Its name survives, but only just, as a short section opposite Clifford Street. Not much found its way into the street directories until the 1850s, the earlier 1840s entries being mainly along the north side between Nightingale Court and Cross Street. The numbers ran from the St Mary Street end along the south side as 1 to 37 to Cossack Street, then returned along the north side as 38 to 78 back to St Mary Street.

CRAVEN STREET – SOUTH SIDE NOS. 1 TO 11

Most of Craven Street dates back to the 1850s, with No. 1 being home to John Young who was a baker and beer retailer around 1860. After that it appears to have been a residence until the mid-1880s when it no longer featured in the directories. No. 2 was always a residence and was occupied by Harry Messinger from the early 1900s until the street was cleared. No. 3 was possibly No. 2A at one time and

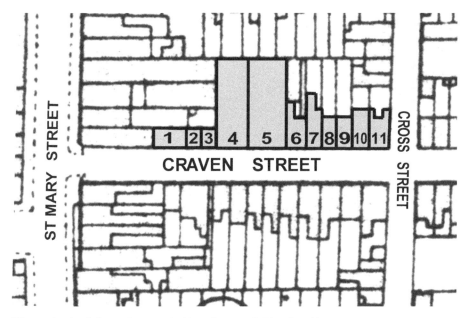

The south side of Craven Street at St Mary Street with Nos. 1 to 11.

was occupied by butcher Harry Rowbotham before becoming Brown Brothers upholstery works.

The 1891 census states that houses 3, 4 and 5 had been redeveloped as corn stores. No. 4 was previously the home of wheelwright Robert Brown in the 1880s but afterwards became the premises of corn and coal merchants Knowlton and Sons, who were there until the mid-1920s. They also briefly occupied No. 4 until it became the property of salt merchant Henry Stride, at which time Knowlton & Sons moved to No. 5, which was shared between the two firms from World War One. Knowltons moved out in about 1910 and then Stride's salt works occupied both Nos. 4 and 5 until demolition came.

No. 6 was a house occupied by tin-plate worker William Lemon in the 1860s and Harry Olive was its final tenant from the mid-1920s. In the early days, No. 7 was occupied by John Frampton during the 1860s, John at first being a boot maker and then becoming a coach builder. Some of the more interesting later tenants were lamp lighter Edward Sainsbury, pilot John Hodges and music professor Sydney Franz Leipzig. Back in the 1860s, No. 8 was the abode of laundress Elizabeth Lenny before Elizabeth Warren moved in and became a general dealer and shopkeeper from the 1870s until the 1880s. It then became a residence occupied for many years by the Hayward family from World War One until the early 1930s.

Craven Street, Nos. 6 to 11 on the south side looking towards Cross Street.

In 1851 No. 9 was the home of steamboat fireman Joseph Broomfield. The Russell family took up that address in the early 1880s and ran their boot-making business there through to the end. Nos. 10 and 11 were a general shop run by Thomas Collins from the 1870s, but by the early 1900s John Edward Winstanley had taken over and began selling beer there until it reverted to a grocery shop in the mid-1920s and continued as such in the remaining years.

CRAVEN STREET – SOUTH SIDE NOS. 12 TO 29

Nos. 12 to 29 between Cross Street and Winchester Place were houses, mainly occupied by labourers, but with a few tradesmen amongst them consisting of plasterers, carpenters, slaters and painters, no doubt all employed in the house building that was happening in the early years. Bricklayer John Bartlett was at No. 19 from the 1850s until the 1870s.

Several long-term tenants saw out the final decades of the street. James Macey was resident at No. 12 from World War One and Tom Ricketts, at No. 15, was there even

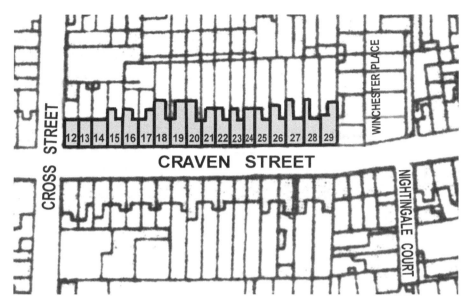

Numbers on the south side of Craven Street ran from 12 to 29 between Cross Street and Winchester Place.

longer, having moved in during the early 1900s. James Stone at No. 18, Harry Gardner at No. 19, William Baddams at No. 20 and the Shotters at No. 21 were all veteran stayers

Craven Street south side Nos. 12 to 29 from the junction with Cross Street.

Looking east along the south side of Craven Street, showing Nos. 29 to 20. No. 1 Winchester Place is the nearest building on the right.

and painter Daniel Mabey lived in No. 24 from 1900 until the end, having previously lived at No. 28. With the Marlows at No. 27 and the Painters at No. 29, also there for generations, it must have been a very close-knit community.

CRAVEN STREET – SOUTH SIDE NOS. 30 TO 37

Nos. 30 to 36 were originally numbered 1 to 8 in the opposite direction until about 1870. Mrs Ann Bowers lived in No. 30 as one of the earliest tenants through the 1860s (she had previously run a beer house at No. 60 in the 1840s). Ships steward James Weldon was there from 1871 and his family remained at that address for generations until Thomas Weldon was the last occupant in the 1930s. The Fox family were in No. 31 from 1912 until at least 1931 and, from the 1870s, there was a No. 31A next door with a narrow passage that led to the Mission Cottages (described later). The Pothecarys were resident in No. 32 from the early 1900s until the end. Laundress Matilda Easter was in No. 33 throughout the 1860s to 1880s, after which Mrs Reid was there for

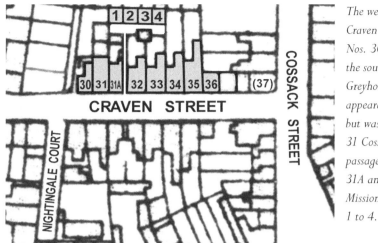

The western end of Craven Street with Nos. 30 to 36 on the south side. The Greyhound pub often appeared as No. 37 but was, in fact, No. 31 Cossack Street. The passage between Nos. 31A and 32 led to the Mission Cottages Nos. 1 to 4.

the same period as the Pothecarys next door. The 20th century saw George Seal move into No. 36, giving way to Sidney Macey from the time of the First World War until the 1930s when he moved to No. 34. No. 37 is shown in the directories as being the *Greyhound* pub, which was also listed as No. 31 Cossack Street (which see).

No. 35 to 30 on the south side of Craven Street looking east from Cossack Street. The rebuilt Greyhound pub is on the right.

WINCHESTER PLACE

The five houses of Winchester Place and the four of Surrey Place between Craven and Winton Streets.

WINCHESTER PLACE NOS. 1 TO 5

Winchester Place was a group of five houses off Craven Street, almost opposite Nightingale Court. Each had a large front garden but very little space at the rear. The earliest occupants appeared in the 1841 census and were engineer Andrew Oliver,

Nos. 1 to 5 Winchester Place had large front gardens for the area.

labourer John Donkin and gardener Benjamin Myall. The final occupants in the 1930s were Charles Edmonds at No. 1, Frank Moores at No. 2, Mrs L. Fox at No. 3 along with Frank Blanchard, who had lived at No. 4 since around 1912, and dredger-engine driver Henry Cross who had moved in to No. 5 at the turn of the century.

CRAVEN STREET – MISSION COTTAGES

These four cottages, known earlier as Edmond's Court, were accessed through a narrow passage between Nos. 31A and 32 Craven Street. As with many of these little houses, all the windows and doors were at the front with no back yard and certainly no through-ventilation where air could circulate through the buildings. Numbered 1 to 4, they were well over 100 years old by the time these photographs were taken in 1935, shortly before the demolition of the whole Kingsland area – and probably not before time – but at least they were homes for somebody. The housing report of 1893 describes them as dark, but in fair condition with their water supply, lavatories and an ash pit outside in the yard.

Looking east along the former Edmond's Court at Nos. 1 to 3 Mission Cottages.

The other direction at the Edmonds Court showing Nos. 2 to 4 Mission Cottages.

The 1851 directory shows just three tenants at Edmonds Court, these being labourer Joseph Heathcote, bricklayer George Ward and blacksmith Donald Mackay. By the early 1900s, Abel Jeffries and his family had moved into No. 1 and stayed on until the end. The Griffin family moved into No. 3 at a similar time and remained there until the 1920s, and the final resident at No. 4 was William Street, who had lived there since World War One.

CRAVEN STREET – NORTH SIDE NOS. 38 TO 46

Nos. 38 and 39 stood alone on the corner at the Cossack Street end and in 1851 were the abodes of general dealer George Pembroke and coach painter William Gray. By 1891, shoe maker Benjamin Curd (who crops up several times around Kingsland) had moved into No. 38, where Sidney Vincent was the last occupant, having lived there since the First World War. Joseph Peachey was in No. 39 even longer, having taken up residence there by 1907.

No. 40 saw many arrivals and departures in the early years, including bricklayer Joseph Hinves, tailoress Mary Ann Dolan, gardener Daniel Painter and cooper John

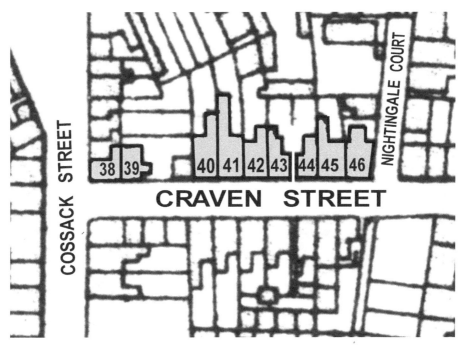

Nos. 38 to 46 on Craven Street's north side near Cossack Street.

Nos. 40 to 46, with the shop at No. 41, on the north side of Craven Street, looking east from Cossack Street towards Nightingale Court.

Henry, before Benjamin Fargher arrived in the early 1900s and remained until the end. No. 41 was always a shop, originally run by baker Robert Swift. Other bakers plied their trade there before James Frederick ran it as a general store in the 1880s. A succession of shopkeepers followed, including John William Maxted, from the First World War until the early 1930s, then finally James E. Shotter became the last of a very long line to trade there.

Wheelwright William Edmonds and his family were at No. 42 from around 1860 until the 1880s, having previous lived at No. 55 since the 1840s. William George Grice moved in during the Great War and was one of the final residents. Similarly, greengrocer William Smith at No. 43, Harry Mitchell at No. 44, and the Wilkins family at No. 45 were also there for an equal period.

No. 46 on the corner of Nightingale Court was at one time a pub named the *Carpenters Arms*. Back in the 1850s it had been a shop run by Harriet Beale, but from 1866 it was selling beer under landlord Charles Jacobs, a carpenter by trade, hence the name. Leased to the Winchester Brewery it had several licensees names over its door before closure came in 1911, after which it reverted back to a shop with Harry Harris being its final keeper.

CRAVEN STREET – NORTH SIDE NOS. 47 TO 67

Thomas Northover lived at No. 47 and earned a living as horse breaker and groom. The Biggs family lived there from the 1890s until the First World War and William Lawler was there for the last decade. Dress maker Annie Fenton was at No. 49 in the 1870s and the final occupant there was Robert John Williams for the final 15 years. Coachman Frederick Redman occupied No. 50 in the 1860s before William Collins had a long stint there from the early 1900s until the mid-1920s. Furniture movers were prevalent at No. 51, with William Gigg plying his trade in the 1870s and William Painter during the following two decades. He was followed by the Ellery family, who lived there from the turn of the century until demolition came. Soloman Beare was another long-term tenant at No. 52, being in residence from the Great War until the street's final days.

Everybody needs a run of luck and a pub of that name evolved at No. 53 in the 1860s when sawyer John Barnes began serving beer from the Winchester Brewery until the

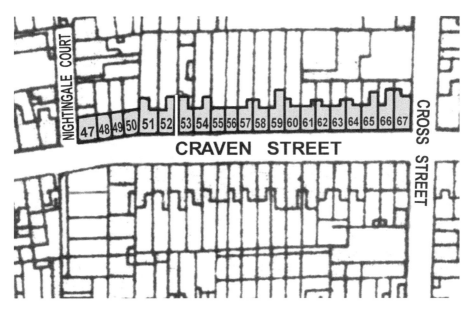

The north side of Craven Street showing Nos. 47 to 67 between Nightingale Court and Cross Street. No. 53 was at one time the Run of Luck pub.

1870s when it became a general shop run by his wife. But the *Run of Luck* had arisen once again by 1887 under beer retailer Arthur Rose, continuing under several publicans until it was refused a licence in 1910. The building once again became a shop and remained so until the 1920s under Robert Pollard. No. 54 probably had the least number of tenants in the street, with bricklayer William Nutbeam living there from the 1850s until the 1870s, followed later by Frederick Hunt, who was resident from around 1890 until the very end.

This section of the street contained some of its oldest buildings dating back to the 1830s and had some of its earliest inhabitants. Wheelwright William Evans was one of these, having lived at No. 42 from the 1840s until around 1860 when he moved to No. 55. Another early arrival in Craven Street was tailor John Kendall, who lived at No. 56 from the 1840s until at least 1876. Mariner John Gigg lived in No. 57 in the 1850s but had decided to remain ashore from the 1860s when he became an ostler. He was succeeded there by dock labourer William Lockyer and his family until another seaman, Alfred Seaborn, arrived in the 1890s.

George Wheatland set up shop as a shoe maker at No. 58 as far back as 1836, but by 1845 he had turned his hand to selling groceries there. A later tenant was charwoman

Looking east along Craven Street from Nightingale Court to St Mary Street. The shop on the left is No. 46 and was once the Carpenters Arms.

Mary Wareham in the 1870s and 1880s, with the final occupants being the Smith family from about 1912. Porter William Axford was at No. 59 in the 1840s, with William White and his family there from the early 1900s through to the end.

No. 60 was a beer house under R. Batchelor in 1836 and remained so under Ann Bowers in the 1840s. An assortment of painters, glaziers, shipwrights and labourers followed until sawyer James Andrews had a long stint there from 1901 until the mid-1920s, when Charles Brown was last in line there.

Nos. 61 to 67 housed the usual assortment of boot makers, seamen and labourers, but there were several tradesmen amongst them with shipwrights, carpenters, plumbers, painters, bricklayers, sawyers and a stone mason. The Rogers at No. 63, Baileys (No. 64), and the Cutlers (No. 65) were all long-term neighbours in the 20th century. W. Luffman at No. 66 was with the Town Quay Police in the 1880s and the Primmer family ran a grocery shop at No. 67 in the 1840s.

CRAVEN STREET – NORTH SIDE NOS. 68 TO 78

This section of Craven Street's north side, running towards St Mary Street, began with No. 68 on the corner of Cross Street. This was at one time the Free House Inn under Panton's Wareham Brewery from 1843 until 1892, when the Southampton constabulary opposed renewal of its licence, there being too many establishments of this type in the area. William Smith and James Richard Moore were its final landlords and Harry Olive occupied it for the rest of its days as a dwelling, from around 1912 until demolition came.

Builder Joseph Bampton lived at No. 71 from the 1830s. A carpenter by trade, he remained there until the 1870s, no doubt engaged with others in the construction of the local houses. Chimney sweep Frederick Callaway and his family had moved in there by the early 1900s and remained until the end.

George Glasspool lived at No. 75 from the 1850s to the 1870s. George moved around Kingsland and had several addresses in his time. He, and other members of the family, were local lamp lighters. Elizabeth Oakley was at No. 77 in the 1850s and 1860s, surviving on Parish Relief, and painter Frederick Oakley was the breadwinner at that address from 1871. Next door, No. 78 was home to various labourers, shoe makers and an upholsterer before James Thomas Andrews became its final tenant from 1916.

The north side of Craven Street between Cross Street and St Mary Street showing Nos. 68 to 78. No. 68 was once the Free House Inn.

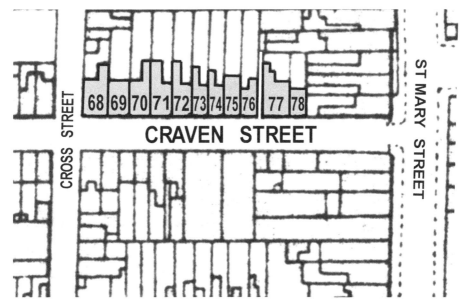

NIGHTINGALE COURT

NIGHTINGALE COURT – NOS. 1 TO 9

Nightingale Court ran off the north side of Craven Street between Nos. 46 and 47. In the early registers there were nine properties but these had been reduced to just four by the end of the 19th century. They did, however, retain their original numbers, so Nos. 1 and 7 to 9 survived until demolition in the 1930s. Communal water and lavatories were available in the court and the condition of the houses was described as fair in the 1893 survey.

In the 1851 census the occupants of Nos. 1 to 9 were blacksmith Henry Osley, porter Francis Thackham, horse keeper James Cox, mariner William Hart, shoe maker George Broomfiend, porter Henry Walton, stay maker Ann Matthews, ostler Frederick Fielder and dress maker Mary Ann Primmer. Each of these dwellings had a high turnover of occupants with a great variety of employment, including sawyers, a hay maker, bricklayers, painters, wheelwrights and an agricultural labourer. Nos. 5 and 6 seem to have disappeared after 1871 and the final tenant in No. 2 was painter George Ricketts in 1891, with coal porter Albert Pothecary being the last recorded inhabitant

The final houses of Nightingale Court off Craven Street

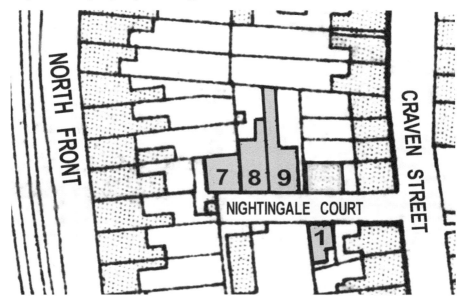

of No. 3 in 1901. When the remaining houses were finally cleared the final roll call was Mrs M. Lovejoy at No. 1, John Walter Street at No. 7, Thomas Henry Marlow at No. 8 and Sidney Alfred Green at No. 9.

WINTON (WINCHESTER) STREET

Dating Back to the 1820s, Winton Street, previously named Winchester Street, was one of the longer roads in Kingsland, running east to west from St Mary Street to West Front (now Palmerston Road), passing Cross Street, Broad Street, Cossack Street and Middle Street along its route. Until the 1860s it was divided into Upper, Middle and Lower Winchester Street, with each section having its own numbering (or lack of) until around 1870 when a more uniform system saw the south side become Nos. 1 to 30 from St Mary Street to Palmerston Road and Nos. 31-78 running back along the north side.

WINTON STREET – SOUTH SIDE NOS. 1 TO 11

The first line of buildings along the south side of the street were Nos. 1 to 11 between St Mary Street and Cross Street. No. 1 was home to the Shuttler family, where head of the house Andrew earned a living as a gardener in the 1850s. His wife Elizabeth outlived him and continued as a dressmaker for two decades longer. By the early 1900s, Misslebrook & Weston had a warehouse on this site. No. 2 seems to have disappeared

The south side of Winton Street at the St Mary Street end with Nos. 1 to 11.

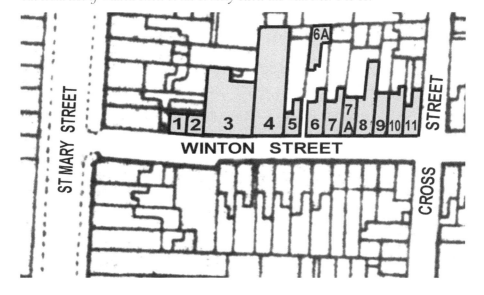

by the mid-1880s when labourer William Over was in residence and it was also taken over by M&W.

Nos. 3 and 4 had suffered the same fate by the 1880s. Both became the wholesale grocer's stores of James Edney & Co from World War One until the firm of Stewart Ltd took over the business in the 1920s. Chimney sweep John Collett was in No. 5 during the 1850s and No. 6 was home to a succession of sweeps from Stephen Mattock in the 1840s and 1850s, with John Moxon hoisting the brushes from the 1850s continuously into the 1880s. William John Smith was the final tenant from 1912 until the street was demolished.

No. 6 saw a varied succession of tenants, including yet another chimney sweep in Frederick Callaway during the 1880s. There was a passage between Nos. 5 and 6, leading to No. 6A (or 6½) at the rear. This was referred to as Brown's Court in the early census returns, with George Downs being the final resident in the 1930s. No. 7 saw Cave Edward Brown as a long-term resident from the early 1900s until the very last days of the street. He was equalled by William Wilmer Holmes, who occupied No. 8 for the same period.

On the corner of Cross Street stood No. 11, which was a shop from at least the 1860s when Ellen Williams ran it as a grocer's. For a while, in the 1870s and 1880s, it was George Wareham's butcher's shop before reverting to a general store under Henry Knowlton and finally Robert Cooper from the early 1900s until demolition came.

WINTON STREET – SOUTH SIDE NOS. 12 TO 19

From the 1870s, No. 12 was home to baker Edwin Woodman and his family until the early 1900s when Frederick Maiden and his folks moved in. Afterwards, Mrs Maiden was on the rent book from the 1920s through to the end. At No. 13, Alfred Cooper, along with Henry Nolan at No. 14 and Edwin John Chaffin at No. 15, were also long-term residents, being there from the early 1900s until the final days.

No. 17 was a pub named the *White Horse* dating from the 1830s when James Newman and his family ran it until around 1870. In the 1880s it was extended into No. 18 and, after a few other landlords had been in charge, the pub served its last pints later that decade and became private residences. No. 17 was occupied by Joseph Read from the

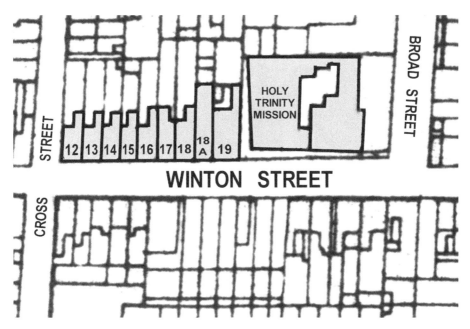

Nos. 12 to 19 and the Holy Trinity Mission on the south side of Winton Street between Cross Street and Broad Street. No. 17 was once the White Horse pub.

Looking west along Winton Street from Cross Street with Nos. 12 to 19 on the left (south) side.

The Holy Trinity Mission in Winton Street was built in 1882 and is now a community centre.

First World War onwards and No. 18 by Earnest Frederick Smith and family for the same period.

An infants' school stood near the corner of Broad Street from 1851, and school mistress Mary Ann Hoadley lived next door at No. 19 in the 1870s. Her house had previously been home to cabinet maker James Beasant (or Bessant) since the 1850s. It was later occupied by dairymen John Minns and David Annett before the Sandy family moved in from the early 1900s and remained until the final days.

The school building gave way to the Holy Trinity Mission Rooms around 1870 and in the 1880s became the Kingsland Workmen's Reading Rooms. A new mission building was erected in 1882 and still stands in modern-day Kingsland, where it now serves as a community centre.

WINTON STREET – SOUTH SIDE NOS. 20 TO 30

This section between Broad Street and Cossack Street was mainly residential, with a shop at No. 29. Coal merchant George Burt lived at No. 21 in the 1840s but by 1851

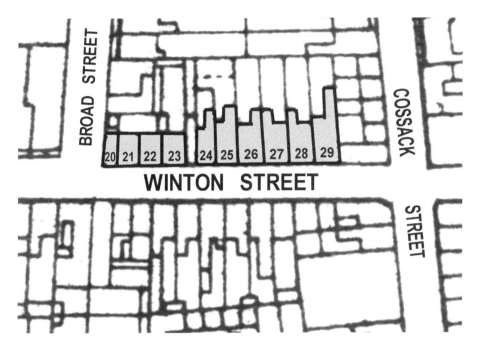

Nos. 20 to 29 on the south side of Winton Street.

he was working as a painter. Charwoman Jane Cotton lived there in 1881 and Frederick Charles Beach was its final occupant, having been there since at least 1912. Charles Herbert Chainey was the final tenant in No. 23, having been in residence since before World War One.

John Bessant, previously at No. 19, had moved into No. 24 during the 1880s and, together with his son John Bruce Bessant, combined their cabinet-making skills to set up a family business as undertakers. William Edward Holmes had taken over the rent book by 1912 and also saw out the remainder of the street's time there. Whitesmith George Sanders was at home in No. 25 through the 1860s and 1870s, after which railway signalman George Hopkins moved in and the Wellman family were the final occupants from the time of World War One.

Monthly nurse Mrs Mary Ann Holloway lived in No. 26 from 1871 until the 1880s and her daughter remained there until the First World War. Then Charles Henry Gilfoy saw out the rest of the house's time. At No. 27 William Knowlton worked at upholstery during his time there in the 1870s and 1880s. Back in the 1860s and 1870s, the Fripp family ran a greengrocer's shop at No. 29. By the 1880s they had changed to become

No. 30 Winton Street looking east towards Middleton Street.

a grocery store until Charles Jeffries took over and began selling beer. It remained as a beer house for many years under E. A. Lovibond until it once again became a grocery shop in the 1930s, with Bertie Charles Wheeler behind the counter. No. 30 was a three-storey building isolated between Middleton Street and Palmerston Road, where Alice Elkins was running it as a boarding house in 1901. Henry Vaughan was the final tenant from the 1920s.

WINTON STREET – NORTH SIDE NOS. 31 TO 39

Nos. 31 to 39 ran on the north side of Winton Street, between Palmerston Road and Cossack Street. No. 32 was briefly a pub named the *Lord Derby Inn* run by John Wingham back in 1869. Having previously been the home of seaman Samuel Porter, its time as a pub was short lived and the building had reverted to a dwelling once again by 1871. Railway porter William Aldridge was at No. 34 in the 1860s, while painter and glazier John Webber lived next door at No. 35 also during the 1860s and into the 1870s. William Read was its final occupant from the outbreak of World War One until the street was

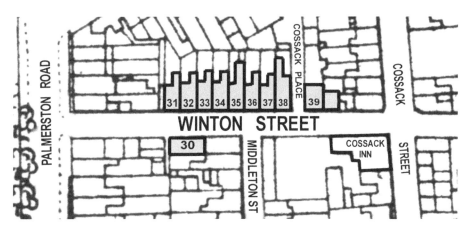

The west end of Winton Street with No. 30 on the south side and Nos. 31 to 39 opposite.

demolished. Edmund Taylor was working as a bricklayer while living in No. 36 in the 1850s, and by the 1870s he was still there, having also developed the skill of plastering.

No. 37 had china dealer Nathaniel Beckley living there back in the 1840s. By the 1950s it was home to flour man James Clarke and then blacksmith James Plumley in the 1860s and 1870s. No. 38 had been the abode of a blacksmith, boot maker, gentleman's servant and several labourers before William Williams held the keys from the early 1900s until the street fell.

Nos. 38 to 31 Winton Street looking west towards Palmerston Road with the entrance to Cossack Place on the right.

No. 39 Winton Street viewed from the yard of the Cossack Inn. Back in the 1850s this was at one time the Bakers Arms pub. The store on the right was once used by a blacksmith and a bricklayer.

No. 39 (previously No. 9 Winchester Street under the old numbering) stood at the entrance to Cossack Place since at least the 1840s when it was a shop run by Mrs Mary Primmer. By 1851 baker John Young had taken over and ran it as a grocery store, then in the 1853 directory he was listed as beer retailer at the *Bakers Arms*. Samuel Roo was at that same address in the 1860s as a painter and beer retailer, but by the 1870s it was back to being a shop again with Mrs Emma Penny selling second-hand clothes there. Afterwards it became a grocer's shop once more, into the early 1900s, but by the 1920s it was merely a residence.

WINTON STREET – NORTH SIDE NOS. 40 TO 50

As far back as 1843, No. 40 Winton Street, on the corner of Cossack Street, had been a pub (see also No. 13 Cossack Street). At first named the *Soldiers' Return* under the stewardship of plasterer William Kemmish, it came under the ownership of Welsh's Lion Brewery from 1867. By 1871 it had extended into No. 41 and was renamed the

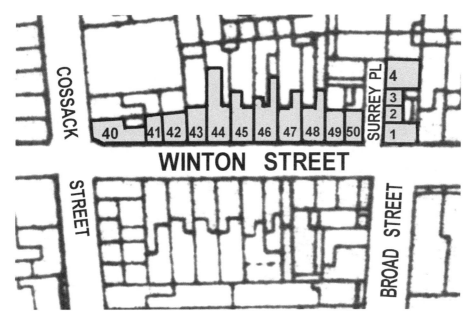

Nos. 40 to 50 Winton Street and Nos. 1 to 4 Surrey Place.

Ship and Anchor under Scrace's Star Brewery. After several changes of landlord, the last being William Leggett, it closed in 1906 and became a general shop run by Mrs Smyth until the 1920s. Its final occupant was wholesale newsagent Spencer W. Duggins.

From 1841 No. 42 had the usual smattering of carpenters, sawyers, a laundress and a porter, with Walter O'Brien living there in the final decade. Initially, the tenant at No. 43 was cow keeper John Bruce, but by the mid-1840s it had become a greengrocer's shop under Nehemiah Hookey, who was a market gardener by trade. Hookey cultivated 3.5 acres of land to produce his vegetables, until Henry Norris took over in the 1870s. The shop continued in greengrocery until Joseph Thomas changed it to a sweetshop, but by 1916 it had reverted to a greengrocer's under Mrs Annie Thomas, with Mrs Brown being the final custodian.

Baker James Croucher resided at No. 44 from the 1850s until the 1880s and the Edmondson family were the last at that address from 1920, having previously lived next door at No. 45. Gentleman Edward Butler was in No. 46 during the 1860s, while painter and plumber William Bryant had the tenancy from 1871 until the late 1880s, prior to the White family seeing out the remainder of the house's existence from 1914. Plasterer John Barber and his family had lived at No. 47 from the turn of the century

Nos. 50 to 40 on the north side of Winton Street, viewed from the corner of Broad Street. Surrey Place is on the right where the women are standing. In the distance is No. 40 on the corner of Cossack Street, once the Ship & Anchor pub.

until the very end. Mrs Harriet Dimmick was a charwoman at No. 48 in 1861, but a decade later, and for the next ten years, she was recorded as being a nurse. Builder's carter John Callaway had moved in by 1901 and was there until the 1920s, Ernest Bert Reed having taken over in the 1920s as the final householder.

No. 49 was one of those houses that never seemed to attract any lingering tenants, with different names appearing with each directory or census. Railway porters, blacksmiths, boot and shoe makers along with several labourers all came and went from the 1840s until Alfred Wild became the last of the line from the 1920s onwards. No. 50 on the corner of Surrey Place was deemed only a little more attractive, with seamstress Marion Smith, in the 1860s, and boiler maker William Moger, in the 1870s, being some of the few who stayed on for any length of time. Mrs Green was the last resident in the 1930s.

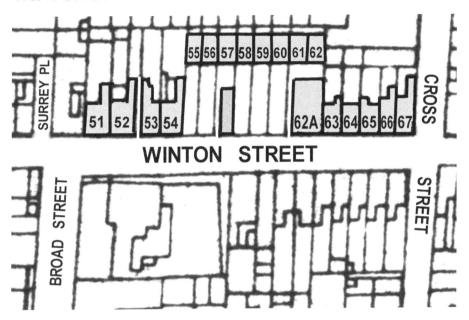

The houses between Surrey Place and Cross Street, where Nos. 55 to 62 were once known as The Gardens.

Nos. 51 to 67 were between Surrey Place and Cross Street on the north side of Winton Street. No. 51 was home to carpenter and joiner Stephen Peters in the 1850s, followed by railway porter George Philpot in the following decade. Next door at No. 52 were the Pointer family in the 1860s, where Pricilla Pointer was a recipient of Parish Relief. James Woodling was its final occupant from the early 1900s until the final days.

Blacksmith George Colmer and his dressmaker wife graced No. 53 in the 1860s until fellow smith, Robert Lambert, took over the tenancy in 1871. The Knowlton family were at No. 54 for a lengthy spell from the 1870s until the 1930s, George being a labourer to a coachman and Thomas being a carman.

In the 1861 census Nos. 55 to 62 were known as Nos. 1 to 8 The Gardens, presumably as they all had substantial (of the day) front gardens – all apart from Nos. 62 and 63, which were overshadowed by 62A, a building that was J. C. Dyas sail maker's store in 1914 and then became Cave & Co's wine & spirits warehouse in the mid-1920s. Similarly, at No. 57 the Brown family ran a wood and coal business from the 1880s to the early 1900s and had a workshop in front of their house, which was later occupied

Nos. 58 to 61 Winton Street were once Nos. 4 to 7 in a small terrace known as The Gardens that were overshadowed by the store on the right of the photo that was No. 62A.

by decorators Penfold Brothers in the 1920s. Albert Tall (No. 58), Charles Snook (No. 59) and Mrs Hansford at No. 60 were all final long-term tenants for most of the 1900s.

Nos. 63 to 37 were homes to wheeler Henry Sanger, plasterer George Scorey, brewer John Mitchell and bricklayer George Rogers in the 1850s. There followed the usual collection of tradesmen, seamen and labourers, before Thomas Addison appeared in 1914 and remained for the rest of the street's existence. Boot repairer Benjamin Curd and his family crop up in several of Kingsland's streets over the years, and on this occasion they were at No. 64 from the early 1900s until the First World War, while labourer George Holloway and his family lived in No. 65 from around 1905 and through the final three decades.

Of the longer inhabitants at No. 66, shipwright Richard Riddett's family were there from the early 1880s until at least 1907. George Harnett, a shore trimmer on the White Star Line, was in No. 66 through World War One before William Trethgarthen saw out the final 15 years there. William had previously lived next door at No. 67 during the war.

WINTON STREET – NORTH SIDE NOS. 68 TO 78

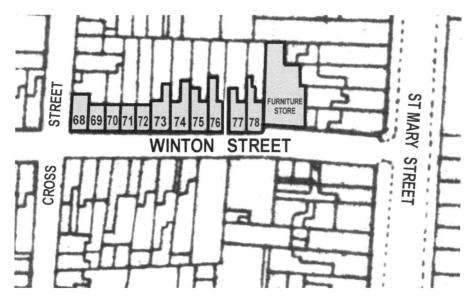

The north side of Winton Street with Nos. 68 to 78 towards St Mary Street. Nos. 68 and 69 were the Waggoners Arms pub.

Unfortunately, I have yet to come across any photographs of this part of the street, but the *Waggoners Arms* pub stood at Nos. 68 and 69 on the corner of Cross Street. They were originally private residences until Welsh's Lion Brewery took out a 21-year lease on them in 1866, with Thomas Hardy being an early landlord. It was afterwards taken over by Perkins' Globe Brewery when one of the licensees was Charles Henry Gates who ran the pub during and after World War One. In its final years the pub had come into the hands of Brickwoods when it closed due to the area being cleared. Walter Pearson was the final publican.

Charles Henry Gates with his wife Isabella, who ran the Waggoners Arms in Winton Street through World War One and into the 1920s (Courtesy of David Dawkins).

Latter day Winton Street where it meets Broad Green.

John Stephen Davis lived at No. 70 from the early 1900s, while the Judd family were in No. 73 from around 1880 until the street came down, beginning with Mark Judd, a stone cutter and finally window cleaner William Judd in the 1930s. From the 1840s, Henry Homer occupied No. 77, working as shopkeeper, chandler and finally as a chimney sweep in the 1870s. William Thomas Painter was the final tenant in that house, having moved there in the early 1900s. Next to No. 78 was a large store which was occupied by the Russell & Sons furniture company from around the turn of the century.

COSSACK PLACE

COSSACK PLACE – EAST SIDE NOS. 1 TO 6

Cossack Place was a row of six houses in a small court with entry between Nos. 38 and 39 Winton Street. All except one had no through-ventilation. The ground floors were below pavement level and very damp.

As with many of these small courts, there was a large turnover of occupants through the generations. No. 1 was the haunt of various seamen through the 1860s to 1880s, but after Michael McGuirk arrived there around 1912 he stayed on until the 1920s. An early

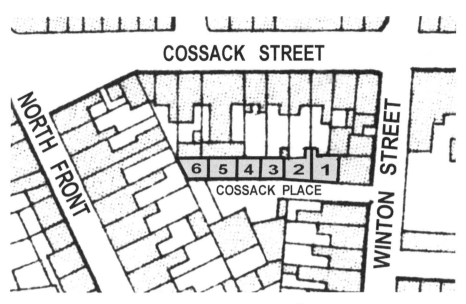

Cossack Place was a row of six houses tucked away in a court off Winton Street.

tenant at No. 2 was P&O ships steward John Townsend. Various labourers came and went before housekeeper Mrs Susan Hammond arrived around the turn of the century. She was gone within a decade, making way for William Smith, who was there until the 1920s. Martin Ernest White was the final occupant through the 1930s.

Cossack Place viewed from No. 39 Winton Street.

More labourers and shipyard workers passed through No. 3 until Edward Julian arrived during Wold War One and remained there until the 1930s. No. 4 was the home of the Pope family from the 1860s. The Hammonds were in residence in the 1880s, then came the Morris family in the early 1900s, before Mrs Self arrived about 1920 and kept house there until the end.

Corn merchant's clerk Benjamin Eames lived at No. 5 in the 1860s and 1870s, followed by the usual turnover of labourers before Mrs Thorn spent three decades there from the early 1900s. Mrs Elizabeth Eames (maybe related to Benjamin next door) was at No. 6 during the 1870s and 1880s. By 1912 Mrs White had taken over for a few years until the Ravenscroft family had the door keys from around 1920 until the last days.

SURREY PLACE

SURREY PLACE NOS. 1-4

Surrey Place consisted of four houses next to No. 50 on the north side of Winton Street. In the early directories it is referred to as Duncan's (or Donkin's) Court, separated from

The four houses of Surrey Place stood next to No. 50 on the north side of Winton Street. No. 1 is nearest.

the adjacent Winchester Place by a high wall which was recommended to be removed in the 1893 survey to improve ventilation. It was described as one of the better courts in the survey, although it had only one common tap in the yard. In the early days it was occupied by seamen's families but by the 1880s it was more diverse, with laundress Harriet Winter at No. 1, lamp lighter and painter James Weaver at No. 2 and seamstress Sarah Aldridge at No. 4. By the 20th century there were long-term residents in Thomas Westbury at No. 2, Arthur Weaver at No. 3 and the Lock family at No. 4, who all stayed until the end.

JOHNSON STREET

Johnson Street is still evident, running off St Mary Street but is a mere echo of its former self. Originally named John Street until 1880, it ran east to west from St Mary Street to Broad Street.

JOHNSON STREET – SOUTH SIDE NOS. 1 TO 15

The 1851 census shows cabin steward John Hedger resident at No. 1. He was followed by Elizabeth Warren, a mason's widow. Labourers, a shipwright and a plasterer followed until a line of Henrys appeared from the turn of the century. First was Henry Biggs, then Henry Porter and finally Henry William Littlehales, who was the last at that address. At No. 2, gardener James Goddard was there for a decade from around 1860. Mariner Henry G. Jocelyn was soon to follow in the 1880s but the 1900s saw a regular turnover of tenants, none of whom stayed very long.

The south side of Johnson Street where No. 6 was a cycle makers and No. 15 was a grocer's shop. No. 11 has access to No. 11A at the rear.

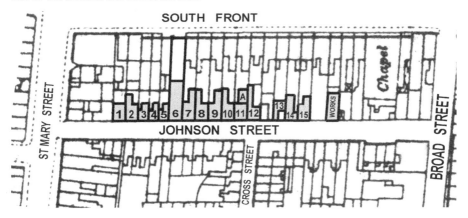

General dealer Eliza Hillier was at No. 3 in the 1850s. Bricklayer William Woods moved in through the 1860s and from then it was the standard mixture of seafarers and boot makers until John Heatley was there from before the First World War until his house was demolished along with the rest of the street.

Further members of the Jocelyn family were in No. 4. John, and Francis and another Henry appeared from the 1850s to the 1870s. I assume this was a different Henry from the mariner at No. 2, as this one was recorded as a cripple. Mrs E. Kelcey was there long term from the outbreak of World War One until the 1930s.

Stonemason George Warren lived at No. 5 in the 1850s but was obviously soon deceased as we have already seen his widow at No. 1. The Long family were resident at No. 5 through the 1870s and 1880s. John Long was a labourer and Henry Long a boot maker. In the 1900s George Rendle had moved in from the time of the First World War and stayed until the end.

No. 6 was described as uninhabited back in the 1850s but by 1861 the Targett family had found a home there and stayed until the 1880s when the building became a store and was then taken over by cycle makers Woodford & Farr in the early 1900s, having extended their premises though from South Front. They remained until the 1920s after which the address disappeared from the directories.

The Goreys featured several times at No. 7. Susan Gorey was a charwoman there in 1851 and labourer George lived there in 1871, along with Susan who was of independent means. Archivers porter and broker Frederick Snellgrove followed the Goreys from the 1870s and was there until the turn of the century. William Giblin was there next until the 1920s with Frederick Ainsworth being its final tenant.

Ships fireman Benjamin Reed and his wife Elizabeth graced No. 8 from the 1860s before bill poster George Cozens stayed there through the late 1870s. In later years, coal merchant William John Spratt spent many years there from around 1912 to at least 1931. No. 9 looks to have been a shop from the 1870s with George Dear and his wife being general dealers and then a greengrocer's until the 1880s when further shopkeepers carried on the business, ending with the Leadbitters from 1925.

No. 10 saw machine labourer Henry Head at home there from the 1850s until the mid-1880s and James Barnaby had a long stint from around 1912 until the 1930s. No.

11 was a little odd in that it had two front doors, the second of which led through to No. 11A at the rear. No. 11 had seen the usual journeymen, labourers and seafarers but No. 11A does not appear until 1881 when the census recorded 'Upton House' as the home of Ann V. Sargent between Nos. 11 and 12. The Thorn Family were there for many years from the early 1900s until at least 1931.

No. 12, facing Cross Street, was always a shop dating back to at least 1861 when John Eggs ran it as a grocer's. Since then it had alternated to other uses, becoming a bakery at times and briefly a marine store in the 1881. It then returned to being a general shop and, after several owners, was run by the Brown Family from around 1912 until William H. Bryant saw out the final years in the 1930s.

Various seafarers inhabited No. 13 from the 1860s to the turn of the century when boiler marker William Turner was there until World War One and Tom Topp moved in. He and his family stayed until the very end. As with many of its neighbours, No. 14 saw the comings and goings of several seamen, but by 1901 parish relief officer John Thorn was the first of a long list of tenants until demolition came.

The south side of Johnson Street with the grocer's shop, No. 12 nearest, running east to No. 1 at the St Mary Street end. No. 11 next to the shop had an extra entrance for access to No. 11A behind it.

No. 15 was a house named *Pembroke Cottage* which, from around 1912, was occupied by Edward Hack until the mid 1920s with Maurice George Judd being the final tenant.

The final building on the south side was the workshop and store of carter and contractor James Avery in the 1880s. After the turn of the century it was an electrical engineer's works run by Wishart & Co until Henry Charles Taplin took over the business after World War One, remaining there until the final days.

JOHNSON STREET – NORTH SIDE

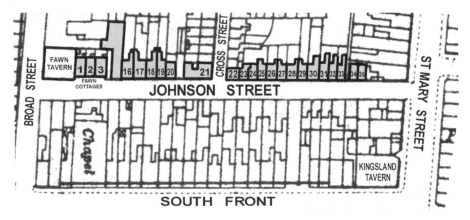

The north side of Johnson Street with the Fawn Cottages and Nos. 16 to 35.

JOHNSON STREET – NORTH SIDE – FAWN COTTAGES NOS. 1 TO 3

The three Fawn Cottages stood on the north side of Johnson Street near its junction with Broad Street. The *Fawn Tavern* on the corner is thought to have taken its name from these. Like the rest of the street, they probably date from the 1830s but did not appear in the directories until the 1870s. The Barfoot family were resident in No. 1 from around 1912 until the final days of the street, while the Goodfellows were in No. 3 almost as long, from about 1914.

JOHNSON STREET – NORTH SIDE NOS. 16 TO 35

The early directories show there was a mineral water factory between Fawn Cottages and No. 16 Johnson Street. This was the premises of A. C. Hattatt & Co, who were there in the 1870s and 1880s. The site later became a slaughter house operated by Walter Olive in the early 1900s. No. 16 was occupied by laundress Ann Gosling in the 1860s and 1870s. In later years the Gilroy family were there from World War One until the street disappeared. Back in the 1860s, No. 17 was the home of prison warder John Russell, presumably engaged at the recently opened gaol in nearby Ascupart Street.

Customs Officer William Stavely resided at No. 18 through the 1860s and 1870s and engine driver, come ships stoker, Charles Knowlton was the key holder from the 1880s until World War One. Alfred James Smith and his family then moved in and remained there until the end. Coachman Joseph King lived in No. 19 from 1851 until 1876, by then a pensioner. In later years, from 1916, Henry Oliver was there for the remainder of the street's existence.

After several early tenants, No. 20 was taken by butcher John Hammond and his wife in the 1870s until dairyman William Witt had arrived in 1881. Henry Isaac Wareham lived there from the 1900s until the 1930s but that address was also shared by a slaughter house at the rear, run by Thomas Ponsford from the early 1900s through to the mid-1920s.

No. 21, on the corner of Cross Street, was a pub named the *Dolphin Inn* (see photo in Cross Street), dating back to the 1870s under licensee William Neale. Its owners, the Winchester Brewery, were refused a licence back in 1906 and the building became a shop under a variety of owners for the rest of its time, ending with George James Skeats. No. 22 was home to a boot maker, a greengrocer and several sweetshop proprietors until Frank Callaway took up residence there and saw out the street's remaining years.

Tailoress Elizabeth Phillips threaded her needles at No. 23 in the 1870s and the longest serving tenant after her was George Dear, there from World War One until the mid-1920s, while next door, at No. 24, the Goodfellows were there even longer, from the early 1900s until the very end. Previous occupants there had been wheelwright John Mears in the 1860s and 1870s and ginger beer carman Robert Read in the 1880s.

Bricklayer's labourer Thomas Nutley lived at No. 25 for two decades from 1851 before making way for railway gatekeeper William King and, a later resident, Mrs Stewart, was there from around 1912 until the mid-1920s. Apart from its original occupant, who was labourer James Mitchell through the 1850s and 1860s, No. 26 saw

A. C. HATTATT & Co.,

VINEGAR DISTILLERS

AND

MINERAL WATER MAKERS.

BY ROYAL LETTERS PATENT.

Soda Water		Potash Water
Seltzer Water		Lithia Water

Sole Licensees for Barrett and Elers' Patent Stoppered Bottles.

FACTORY AND OFFICES—

JOHN STREET, KINGSLAND PLACE,

SOUTHAMPTON.

Hattat's mineral water factory stood on the north side of John Street (later Johnson Street) between Fawn Cottages and No. 16.

Looking east towards St Mary Street from No. 16 to No. 21 Johnson Street. Demolition had already begun beyond Cross Street.

The north side of Johnson Street looking east showing Nos. 22 to 27 from the junction with Cross Street.

no long stayers until Richard Gillard arrived at the turn of the century and remained until the mid-1920s. An assortment of individuals rented No. 27 in its time but the only one to stay any length of time was Mrs Englefield, who was there from the early 1900s until 1916. No. 28 was another abode that failed to keep its occupants, the longest tenant being its last, who was John Henry Pace.

No. 29 was the home of shipwright William Read in the 1870s, but by 1881 tailoress Elizabeth Phillips had moved there from nearby No. 23 but she was gone by the early 1900s when Henry Kiddle and his family arrived and saw out the rest of the street's time. Journeyman builder Richard Todd took up residence at No. 30 around 1851 and, presumably due to the building boom, stayed put until the mid-1870s. Electrician Charles Furzey and his family were there from the turn of the century until the 1920s, when George Lacey was the last tenant.

Hairdresser Henry Witt, who appears elsewhere in this volume, was at No. 31 in the 1850s and 1860s. Baker William Mills abided there in the 1870s and 1880s and he was followed by corn labourer Charles Hinton and his family from around 1900 until the

The eastern end of Johnson Street looking towards St Mary Street and Biglands Bakery shop. The houses shown are Nos. 32 to 35 leading up to the Dorsetshire Arms.

last days of the street. After several earlier tenants, cane chair maker George Masters practised his art at No. 32 for a very long period, stretching from the 1880s until at least 1920. Dock labourer Thomas Harvey had arrived at No. 33 by 1881 and was there until the turn of the century. Albert Edward Millard was the final name in the rent book at that house from 1920 onwards.

Labourer George Reeves's family were in No. 34 through the 1870s, but John Hiron was longest serving at that address, being in residence from around 1912 until the 1930s. The last house along that side of the street was No. 35, which was another of those that never seemed to hold on to is occupants. Almost every directory and census recorded a different householder there.

CROSS STREET

Running north–south between Johnson Street and North Front, this was originally called Longcross Street until around 1880. There were only a couple of residents recorded in the 1851 census and it wasn't until ten years later that the street was shown more fully populated, especially at its southern end near Johnson Street. At one time this street was the location of a women's prison.

CROSS STREET – WEST SIDE NOS. 1 TO 11

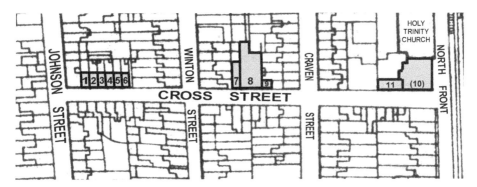

The west side of Cross Street where there was a women's prison on the corner of North Front.

Most of this street's inhabitants were clustered near Johnson Street where there was a corner pub named the *Dolphin Inn* (see Johnson Street). In the 1851 directory, the only residents shown were Mrs Jane Bull and greengrocer William Privett, but the 1851 census records properties Nos. 1 to 9 occupied and five houses empty. No. 1 was a lodging house in the early days kept by Lucy Weeks. At other times it was occupied by a boot maker, coal porter, painter and various labourers, none of whom were around for any length of time, until the arrival of Mrs Proudly, who was there through the First World War until the 1920s.

No. 2 saw a succession of seamen under its roof until the early 1900s when George King set up home there and stayed until the street was demolished. Dressmaker Mrs Sarah Bull was at No. 3 from the 1860s until the 1890s when she was recorded as living on her own means. Thomas Edward Mitchell was one of the longer tenants there, from around 1912 until the mid-1920s. No. 4 was another lodging house in the early days and had a steady turnover of labourers during its existence. Dairyman Henry Stride was an early occupant of No. 5 in the 1860s, after which carter George Hinves moved in until the 1890s. William Reeves was a long-term tenant there from around 1912 until the 1920s when Frederick William Norris moved in and stayed until the end. The last

Demolition was well advanced when this photograph of Cross Street was taken. It shows Nos. 1 to 6 with the former Dolphin Inn on the corner of Johnson Street.

of the terrace was No. 6, which saw a blacksmith, carter and boiler maker's labourer pass through its door until Mrs Lane arrived in the early 1900s and remained until the mid-1920s.

The section of the street between Winton Street and Craven Street was mainly industrial, with coal merchant John Knowlton at No. 7 from the 1920s until the end. At Nos. 8 and 9 was salt merchant Henry Stride, whose family were evident from the 1860s until around 1912. Henry also dabbled with coal and wood for a while. French polisher Edwin White was also at No. 9 from World War One until the final days.

CROSS STREET – WOMEN'S JAIL

At the top of the street's west side, on the corner of North Front, stood a women's jail. Built in 1827, it lasted until 1855 when the new town jail for men and women was built in nearby Ascupart Street. It was referred to as the Female Penitentiary where:

The object of this Institution is to reclaim and to afford an Asylum for females, who, having deviated from the path of virtue, appear penitent and desirous of reform. No person shall be an inmate of the Institution, in a known state of disease, and without evidence of a sincere disposition to reform. The inmates of the Institution shall be employed in washing, and in all the business of a laundry, together with needle and every sort of household work; and that the proceeds of their labour shall be applied towards the current expenses of the Institution. In accordance with the main object of the Institution, the religious instruction of its inmates will be a matter of especial care and attention: and for this purpose a chaplain will be appointed, and a committee of ladies will attend as visitors in rotation.

Ministers of various Christian denominations were expected to preach sermons in aid of fundraising, but by the 1880s it had become a 'Refuge for Fallen Women and Girls'. Then, by the early 1900s, it was known as 'The Refuge for Fallen & Friendless Women', for many years under the guidance of matron Miss E. Rutherford. By the 1930s it had become a lodging house under the name of *Hope Lodge* and the photo shows the buildings in a derelict state in 1941 after wartime bombing.

No. 10 seems to have disappeared in the 1880s, while No. 11 was the home of various sextons attached to the nearby Holy Trinity Church.

The former women's jail on the corner of North Front seen in a derelict state in 1941. Behind is the spire of the war-damaged Holy Trinity Church. The backs of the houses on the right are in New Road.

CROSS STREET – EAST SIDE NOS. 12 TO 23

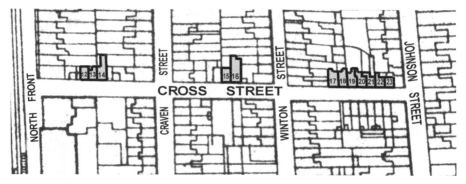

The east side of Cross Street where most of the houses were at the Johnson Street end.

The east side of Cross Street had a trio of houses at the top end near North Front. These were Nos. 12 to 14, and each, over time, housed a variety of mostly unskilled workers. The middle section between Craven Street and Winton Street contained just one house and a store. The house at No. 15 was occupied by several people, including fisherman Thomas Bailey in the 1880s. James Foster moved in around 1912 and remained there until the very end. The store at No. 16 was used by salt merchant Henry Stride, who also had premises opposite at Nos. 8 and 9. After he left, it was an upholstery workshop for a while and finally Henry Rowbottom's butcher's store.

The final terrace of houses on the east side stood between Winton Street and Johnson Street, where a row of seven houses, Nos. 17 to 23, mirrored those opposite. These were homes to a variety of people in the early years. Butcher William Perry was at No. 17 in the 1880s and 1890s, while Richard George Gosling was a long-term resident there from World War One until the mid-1920s

Fireman Henry Phillips lived at No. 18 in the 1870s and a later tenant was Benjamin Foreman, who was there from the early 1900s until John Edward Johnson moved in around 1925 and was its final occupant. Bricklayer's labourer William Felton was living in No. 19 from the 1870s until the 1890s, no doubt fully employed with the local building works during that period, and Mrs Felton was still there by the time World War One broke out. Harry Callaway then became the key holder until the end.

No. 20 saw a relatively stable run of tenants in its time: from boiler maker George Hampton in the 1880s, then Charles Burgoyyne through the early 1900s and finally the

Looking north towards North Front at the top of Cross Street. On the left of the photo is the former women's prison and the tall houses in the distance are those of New Road, across the railway line.

Nos. 16 and 15 on the east side of Cross Street. The off-licence is No. 11 Craven Street.

Nos. 17 to 23 on the east side of Cross Street, looking south to No. 22 Johnson Street.

Hansell family from the mid-1920s onwards. Likewise, No. 21 saw a relatively small turnover of tenants, beginning with journeyman shoe maker Robert, or Rechab Hawkins, who arrived in 1861 and enjoyed his time there so much he stayed until the late 1870s. Edgar Ernest Tall was a street stalwart, being in residence from the early 1900s until the street was cleared.

An early name at No. 22 was cattle dealer William Andrews back in 1861. From the 1870s through to the 1890s, mariner Joseph Follett came ashore there to rest his sea legs before leaving the waves to become a labourer. William Littlehales was the final tenant there in the 1930s. The final house at No. 23 appears to have been vacant through the 1870s, with John George White being the first recorded occupier in the 1880s. John Parsons, through World War One, and then Daniel White from the 1920s, are the only others of note.

BROAD STREET

Broad Street ran north from South Front to Winton Street and had 14 houses, all on the west side of the street. On the opposite side were commercial premises including a pub named the *Fawn Tavern*, which at one time was No. 15, and adjacent was the Malt House Brewery that became a mineral water and bottling factory in later years. After the rebuilding of the area post World War Two, the street was renamed Broad Green.

BROAD STREET – WEST SIDE NOS. 1 TO 14

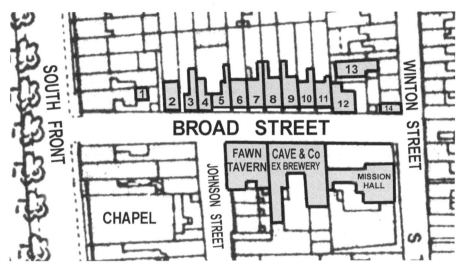

The west side of Broad Street with Nos. 1 to 14, where Nos. 11 and 12 were once a pub named the Pure Drop. Opposite the houses stood the Fawn Tavern and a former brewery.

No. 1 appears to have been a small but tall building set back from the street, backing onto a building in South Front. Mrs Elizabeth Warren was an early resident in the 1840s and ran the address as a lodging house until the 1870s. The Gilroy family had moved in by the turn of the century and remained there until the end. George Street was at No. 2 from the 1840s until the 1880s when he was employed as a bottle washer in a soda water factory. John Thomas was living there in 1916 and stayed until the street came down.

Richard Mears was a cow keeper and labourer back in the 1840s, living at No. 3. John Mears, a brewer, was there a decade later. Labourers, a lamp lighter and a ships foreman came and went before another of the Gilroys moved in. Mrs Gilroy was there until at least 1916 when Frederick Richards became the final tenant. Fireman George Miles was at No. 4 throughout the 1870s and 1880s and Walter Brown was the final occupant, having been there from the First World War until the street was demolished.

In the 1830s, gentleman and rope maker William Thatcher was at No. 5 and his wife Sarah survived him at the house well into the 1870s. James Alfred Luke was another long-term tenant, living there from 1914 until 1925. Mrs Gilroy had moved in there from No. 3 in about 1930 and was the last occupant.

The family of fly and cab proprietor Joseph Boucher had lived at No. 6 from the 1850s. By the 1870s he had become a dock porter and then a dock foreman by the 1880s. His wife Sarah outlived him and survived by her own means until 1901. Joseph Nathaniel Nutburn then moved in until the mid-1920s when Frederick Jeffries became the last occupier at that address. The Flood family were blacksmiths by trade at No. 7, having been there since the 1830s. Adam Flood's son Thomas picked up his father's trade and lived there through the 1840s and 1850s. Labourer George Payne was another long-term tenant there through the 1870s and 1880s, while his tailoress wife Anne lived on until the early 1900s.

More of the Boucher family lived at No. 8 where gas fitter Henry James Boucher was occupier from around 1880 until the mid 1920s, after which Edward Richard Charles saw out the 1930s there as its final occupant.

This unidentified gloomy house set back from Broad Street was very likely No. 1, the lodging house of Mrs Elizabeth Warren.

No. 9 was the home of boot maker Benjamin Sweetingham during the 1850s and 1860s and the next tenant of note was William Veal, who was another fly and cab driver. He was there through the 1870s and Richard Isaacs occupied the house from the turn of the century before handing over to Henry Toswill in around 1920.

Mrs Emma Waldie had previously been at No. 9 but moved to No. 10 in the 1880s. A woman of independent means, she stayed there until at least 1920, after which the Harrison family were the final residents there.

Nos. 11 and 12 were once separate dwellings that later became joined together from the 1870s as a pub named the *Pure Drop*, which was owned by Ashby's Eling Brewery and may previously have been known as the *Slater's Arms*. It was infamous in the 1880s as the scene of a murder where a seaman shot his girlfriend in the bar. Like many others in the area, it was refused a licence in the early 1900s and was closed in 1910. From then on it appeared as a single residence, where Mrs Johnson became the final tenant from 1920 until the end.

No. 13 is something of a mystery as it did not appear in the directories until the 1870s and this was probably a building set back off Broad Street, behind those of South

Nos. 2 to 14 Broad Street looking north along the west side towards Winton Street.

Front. The Tosswill family had a long association with the street. House decorator Harry had moved into No. 13 around the turn of the century but then moved to No. 9 around 1920. His daughter Winfred had become a music teacher by the 1930s. No. 14 does not appear until around 1901 but may have previously been listed as No. 20 Winton Street. Stone cutter John Simms was listed there from the 1880s until the turn of the century, with George Jerram being the final resident there from World War One.

BROAD STREET – EAST SIDE

The east side of Broad Street was not well populated, having only a pub called the *Fawn Tavern* on the corner of Johnson Street, which was well established in the 1830s. At that time, Richard Lock senior was brewing and selling beer in the pub which, in those days, had a brewery next door. His son, Richard Lock junior, carried on the trade into the 1850s. The pub was possibly named after the adjacent trio of Fawn Cottages (see Johnson Street) and belonged to Forder's Hampton Brewery before becoming a Brickwoods house, which traded until closure in 1931. From then the building was no longer in use until its demolition.

On that side of the street, back in the 1880s, was Doggrels Plumbers' Store and Duncan Stubbs the printer. The Brewery in Broad Street is shown on the 1870 map as the Malt House, which, by the turn of the century, had become the premises of Cave & Co, who were mineral water and beer merchants. Caves were joined there by bottlers E. Rendall & Co around 1930, a joint venture that lasted until the street fell. The only other building of note there was the Holy Trinity Mission Hall on the corner of Winton Street.

COSSACK STREET

Cossack Street, running north between South Front to North Front, crossed Winton Street about halfway along. Although it was one of the main thoroughfares through Kingsland, only a few inhabitants were recorded in the 1840s, mainly to the north of Winton Street, at that time known as Winchester Street. At the junction of the two stood the *Cossack Inn*, which dated from the 1820s.

COSSACK STREET – WEST SIDE NOS. 1 TO 12

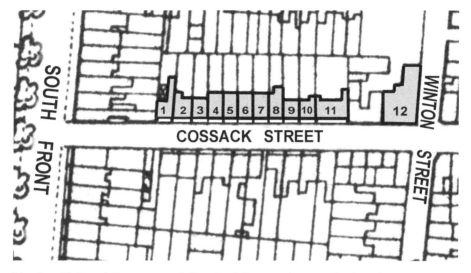

Nos. 1 to 12 Cossack Street ran north from South Front on the west side where there were two pubs. The Rufus Stone at No. 11 and the Cossack Inn at No. 12 on the corner of Winton Street.

Brick burner John Chandler lived at No. 1 Cossack Street during the 1850s and 1860s. At one time there was a building used as a builders' or a greengrocer's store numbered 1A. School mistress Amelia Ireland was at No. 2 in the 1850s, succeeded by blacksmith G. F. Harris in the 1860s and then by various seafarers until George Henry Dent took residence there in the early 1900s and his family remained until the 1930s.

The early residents at No. 3 were the Chalk family, where laundress Mary Ann Chalk scrubbed clothes from the 1840s until the 1860s. Her son Joseph was a letter carrier but took up as a boot closer in the 1860s. Joseph and his sister Caroline remained there until the 1880s. George Moody had a long spell at that address from the early 1900s into the 1920s.

Bricklayer George Light was an early resident at No. 4 until laundress Mary Primmer moved in during the 1860s, and Arthur White was the final tenant there, having arrived during World War One No. 5's only residents of note were Charlotte Godden of independent means in 1841 and tin plate maker James Rogers some 20 years later. Carpenter and joiner James Wellman lived at No. 6 from the 1840s until the 1880s and William Henry Wyman was another long-time inhabitant of that house from around 1914 until the end.

Brush maker Thomas Hayes lived at No. 7 in the early 1840s, a house that was later occupied by bricklayer Henry Isaac from the 1860s until the mid-1870s when his son Joseph was in residence. No. 8 had a great variety of tenants including carpenter Albert C. Wright in the 1860s, butcher Harry Wareham in the 1870s and the lamp lighting Rogers family around the turn of the century. Chimney Sweep Joseph Dicker was the last to live there from the 1920s.

No. 9 was the abode of Joseph Frogley in the 1850s who, having gained a pension from his life at sea, turned his hand to brush making. There were many branches of the Diddams family in Kingsland. Shoe maker Henry was in No. 9 through the 1860s, as was nurse Alice Hubbard in the 1870s. The Flux family had moved in by the 1870s and charwoman Elizabeth Flux was there until the early 1900s. Henry Godwin and his family had taken residence there from around 1912 and saw out the street's final years.

Basket maker Robert Vace was an early inhabitant of No. 10, living there through the 1840s and 1850s. Carpenter Philip Giles and his wife Charlotte were next in line from the 1860s through to the 1880s. By the early 1900s, Charles Munday had taken over the rent book until the 1920s when the Drake family were the last at that address.

Nos. 1 to 12 Cossack Street looking north towards Winton Street.

No. 11 was selling beer back in the 1840s when William Dimond was householder, and by the 1850s it had been named the *Seymour Arms*, with John Diddams behind the bar. By the 1860s its name had changed to the *Rufus Stone* when owned by Forder's Hampton Court Brewery. Seaman George Carpenter and his wife Sarah ran it in the 1870s, before blacksmith Robert Lambert and his wife Mary took over and ruled the roost until the 1880s. The pub lost its licence in 1907 when William J. James was its final landlord and the building became a residence, finally lived in by Edward Sclater.

As one of the oldest buildings in the area, the *Cossack Inn* on the corner of Winton Street dated back to the 1820s when it was run by Elizabeth Pond. It became No. 12 Cossack Street and saw many changes of landlord over its many years, notably George Ovens and his wife Sarah, who ran the pub through the 1870s and 1880s. Owned by Cooper's Brewery, Charles Dorey was in charge in 1917 when the pub was fined for serving out of hours. Dorey was also fined for overcharging in 1922 and it seems the pub had become very run down prior to its closure in 1926. It then became a private residence with its lone tenant in the 1930s being Albert George Pothecary.

COSSACK STREET – WEST SIDE NOS. 13 TO 24

No. 13 Cossack Street is something of a conundrum. On the 1846 map it is shown as the *Soldiers Return* public house but other sources say the pub of that name was the

Nos. 13 to 14 Cossack Street included several shops, one of which may have been a pub at No. 13 named the Soldiers Return.

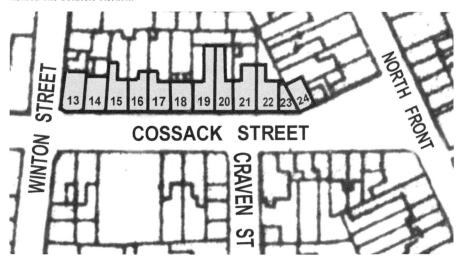

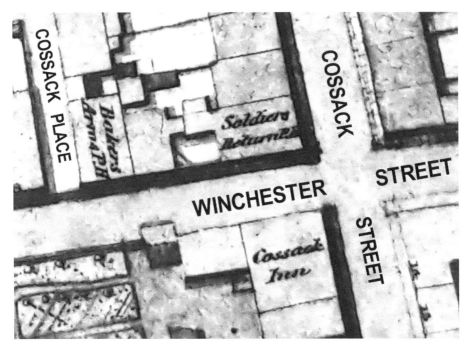

The 1846 map shows No. 13 Cossack Street as the Soldiers Return pub, in good company with the Bakers Arms and Cossack Inn on Winchester (later Winton) Street.

forerunner of the *Ship & Anchor* on the opposite corner, which was Nos. 40/1 Winton Street. The *Soldiers Return* was certainly in existence in the 1840s when plasterer William Kemmish was running it, and No. 13 was always a commercial premises throughout its time. Thomas Yeoman ran it as a grocery shop in the 1870s and 1880s, succeeded by Mr and Mrs Thomas Poore in the early 1900s. One of the final occupants was ice-cream vendor Felix Perrone in the early 1930s.

No. 14 was at times a shop or general residence. Mrs Vear was shopkeeper there in the 1840s, and later, in the 1870s, the Hodges family lived there where Mrs Ellen Hodges sold fruit. By the time of the First World War Ernest Frank Hannay had moved in and by the 1930s he was operating as an undertaker, but despite his keen funeral prices he was never listed as such – always as a cabinet maker.

George Light was another shopkeeper at No. 15 back in the 1840s, and stevedore John Philip Gear lived there from the turn of the century until World War One when greengrocer Albert Pothercary moved in and ran the shop until its final days. Telegraph wire man Anthony Quinn lived at No. 16 from the turn of the century until the First

World War. The Tucker family at No. 17 were plasterers back in the 1840s through to the 1880s and, after a succession of short-term tenants, Charles William Pearce was the last of the line, having moved in during World War One.

No. 18 began life as a greengrocer's shop run by Jeremiah Hookey back in 1841. It was soon to become a general shop under Mrs Mary Andrews through to the 1850s After that, it became a general residence with the usual turnover of labourers, with Albert Victor Grist being the last name on a very long list of householders.

The shop at No. 19 was originally a butcher's run by William Jacobs from 1841, but by the 1870s it had become a grocer's, under the ownership of Mrs Mary Ockleford. The next decade saw a change of use to furniture store under Charles Everett, but by the turn of the century it had reverted to a grocery shop, with Stavely Turner Witt behind its counter from 1912 until the final days.

In 1841 Mrs Mary Bull was at No. 20 where she ran a grocery shop, so successfully that it was trading until the mid 1860s, then through the 1870s it appears to have been a residence until Charles Everett extended his furniture business from No. 19 next door. This lasted into the 1880s, when it became merely a home once again and, as such, saw several tenants pass through until Frederick Yendall became the last, having set up there before the First World War.

Blacksmith George Davidge was one of the early occupants at No. 21 through the 1850s, but by the 1870s Mrs Sarah Lawrence had opened a grocery store there. It was soon changed to a greengrocer's by Adam Longland in the 1880s. He ran the shop until William George Mitchell took over in the early 1900s and remained there until the final days.

The earliest record of No. 22 shows it as a marine store run by Barbary Wiffen, but by the 1850s it had become yet another greengrocer's shop in the charge of James Webb, which lasted until the mid-1860s. Thereafter, it became a private residence that was home to a porter, lamplighter and a tea merchant before ending as the dwelling of William Joseph Murray from 1916 onwards.

The Sparks family had a long association with No. 23, where George Sparks made shoes in the 1840s and his wife Elizabeth ran a lodging house. She outlived him and was still in residence until the 1860s. After her came a long line of various occupants,

*Looking north along the west side of Cossack Street from Winton Street with Nos. 13 to 19.
Many of these were shops at one time or other, while No. 13, where the two children sit, was
possibly the Soldiers Return pub at one time. Ernest Hannay's funeral business was next door.*

Nos. 20 to 24 Cossack Street were opposite Craven Street.

including a carpenter, window-blind maker, plasterer, labourer, boot maker and a house painter. Frederick Meacher, who was there for a decade from around 1916, was the only occupant for any length of time.

No. 24 would seem to have been uninhabited for much of its early existence until labourer Thomas Bread moved in during the 1860s. Grocer's porter Alan Longland was there in the 1870s before moving to No. 21 in the 1880s. An iron borer, ships foreman and a grain porter came and went before Stanley Goodchild Darnell made it his home from around 1912 until the street was no more.

COSSACK STREET – EAST SIDE NOS. 25 TO 36

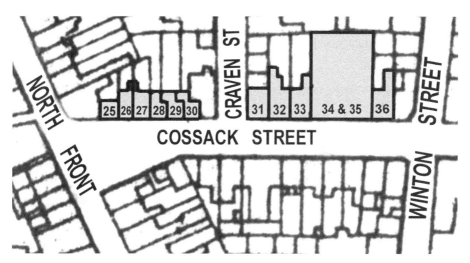

Nos. 25 to 36 Cossack Street where No. 31 was the original Greyhound pub and Nos. 34 and 35 were tallow chandlers works.

The homes along the east side of Cossack Street between North Front and Craven Street also contained another varied collection of occupants dating back to the 1840s, with plasterers, carpenters, cabinet makers and house painters at No. 25. Plumbers, labourers, tailors, dock workers and coal porters lived in No. 26, while No. 27 saw dressmakers, coach makers, lamplighters, carpenters and a baker as residents.

One of the earliest occupants of No. 28 was blacksmith John Melsom, followed over the years by baker John Palmer, ships stoker Alfred Jeffrey, chair maker George Masters, seaman Joseph Spender and coal porter George James Masters.

Labourer William Ingrams was one of the early tenants at No. 29 in 1841, where he resided for a decade. Other labourers followed, as did a laundress, plasterer and a bricklayer, before Edward Charles Betworth moved in during World War One and stayed until the 1930s. Next door at No. 30 saw whitesmith John White as householder in the 1840s and coach smith George Gosling a decade later. A ships fireman, carman and charwoman were among those who passed through in the 1870s and 1880s, but a Mrs Moger was perhaps one of the streets longest-serving tenants, being the key holder there from the outbreak of World War One until the street was demolished.

No. 31 Cossack Street was the *Greyhound* pub which, over the years, also appeared as No. 37 Craven Street. The original pub was in place at least by the 1850s, when Edgar Bugden was in charge. Before that, there is a record of *The Good Intent Beer Shop* run by B. A. Gulliver, which may have been the same premises. Charles Gould was one of its longer-serving landlords and was behind the bar from the 1880s until the 1920s. The pub was rebuilt in Strong's Brewery mock-Tudor in the 1930s, just prior to the streets

Nos. 25 to 30 Cossack Street on the left with Nos. 38 and 39 Craven Street to the right of the photograph. The corner of the Greyhound pub is on the extreme right by the wagon at No. 31 Cossack Street.

The rebuilt Greyhound survived the Kingsland redevelopment but finally succumbed to demolition in 2002.

around it being demolished but, as it was a new building, it was retained as part of the new estate that was built after the Second World War, ending its days in the Whitbread chain before finally being demolished and replaced by a block of flats in 2002.

Nos. 32 and 33 were occupied by mostly unskilled inhabitants, but both saw long-term tenants Mrs Woodward and William Male respectively from the early 1900s. Oddly, both these addresses disappeared from the directories after the 1920s. Nos. 34 and 35 were for many years Smiths Tallow Chandlers, dating from the 1870s, but the business went much further back than that when operated by James Payne in 1847.

No. 36 was always a commercial premises. Richard Gear began as a greengrocer back in 1841 then ran it as general shop before becoming a dealer in various commodities from 1851 until the 1860s. Then by the 1870s it also became a tallow business run by Joseph Clark before he ran a marine store there in the 1880s. By the turn of the century it was a general shop once again, run by Mrs Jane Smythe until it became a boot maker's prior to the First World War under the Spratt family, with Mrs Spratt surviving there until the 1920s.

COSSACK STREET – EAST SIDE NOS. 37 TO 51

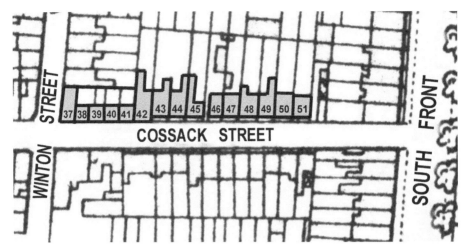

The east side of Cossack Street towards South Front showing Nos. 37 to 51.

This section of Cossack Street dated back to the 1840s and, in its early days, No. 37 was a marine stores belonging to Joseph Williams, but by 1843, and for the rest of the decade and into the 1850s, it was a grocer's shop run by James White and finally Thomas White. Around 1861 it looks to have become a pub named at various times, as *the Running Horse, Soldiers Return* and the *Ship and Anchor*. All are mentioned in this vicinity but the records are somewhat vague. At any rate, it had become a general shop run by Frederick Fripp by the 1880s when it disappeared from Cossack Street and was then listed as No. 20 Winchester (Winton) Street.

All the rest were residences, with No. 38 housing a coach trimmer and a boot maker until butcher Henry Robinson lived there during the 1870s and 1880s, and the tenancy changed hands many times after he had gone. Labourer Thomas Hill was in No. 39 for at least a decade, beginning in 1841. He was followed through the 1860s and 1870s by iron moulder John Townsend. The 20th century saw several more changes until Charles Powell moved in during the 1920s and was the last at that address.

No. 40 was another of those properties that had a different occupant with each directory and census, ending with the wonderfully named George Dragon from the 1920s onwards. No. 41 was the abode of labourers but shown as uninhabited in the 1851 census. Coach trimmer Richard Jackson was there a decade later. He was followed by yet another fine assortment of the local population, including a butcher, a builder's carter and a seaman, before Frederick John Turpin turned up around 1912 and stayed on until the street came down. Originally earning a living as a house painter, William A. Golding, was at No. 42 in 1851. A decade later he was there as a shopkeeper and printer and he remained there until recorded as a retired grocer in 1881. The Ingram family were the final occupants all the way through from the early 1900s.

Nos. 43 to 51 were of three storeys, with the lower floor below street level. The Barnard family were boot makers as far back as 1836, where James earned his living at No. 44 and had become a proprietor of houses by 1861, employing seven men. Two of his sons, James Jnr and Robert continued the boot and shoe business, with Robert operating from No. 43 next door. Robert's son John was the third generation of the family to carry on the tradition. Both branches of the family were there until the 1870s. Absalom Thomas Stewart was a later tenant at No. 44 from the early 1900s until the 1930s

The east side of Cossack Street from South Front towards Winton Street, with No. 51 nearest and No. 38 in the distance. The store on the right may have briefly been No. 52

From the 1850s, No. 45 was at times the home of coachman Richard Flood, butcher Thomas Ponsford and carpenter William Rogers, whose family moved next door to No. 46 around the turn of the century. No. 46 had previously been the home of John Cantell, a contractor's labourer who was there from 1861 and remained in retirement until 1876. In the mid-1830s, No. 47 was the abode of Elizabeth Harden, a stay maker. In the 1860s and 1870s it was the home of Joseph Martin, a quartermaster in the merchant navy, and John Thomas Drake was the final occupant there, having arrived about 1912.

No. 49 was a house of industry, with stone mason Joseph Harris chipping away from the early 1840s and his carpenter son Joseph Scott Harris remaining until the mid-1860s. John Clark was another of the street's long-term final tenants, living there from around 1912. Sharon Cull, a woman of independent means, lived in No. 50 back in the 1840s. In later years, laundress Mrs Mary Ann Howells was resident there from at least 1861 until the mid-1880s. At No. 51, Eleanor Lumsden was another lady of independent means in 1841, but by 1843 that address was a shop run by Mrs Williams until around 1850. She was followed by William Hopkins, a maker of ginger beer there until the mid-1880s. Charles Edward Andrews was the last of three occupants from the turn of the century.

MIDDLETON STREET

Middleton Street was one of the shorter streets in Kingsland, running north from South Front to Winton Street. Until the late 1800s it was known as Middle Street, and although it had only 23 houses along its length, it also had several courts leading off each side. These were Farmers Court and Everett's Courts on the west side and Bromfield Court on the east side. The houses along the western side were numbered 1 to 10 from South Front with Nos. 11 to 23 running back on the opposite side.

MIDDLETON STREET – WEST SIDE NOS. 1 TO 10

Middleton Street's west side began at South Front where, at No. 1, coach smith Joseph Fisher resided in 1851. It was later occupied by the Wray family for much of its existence. Boot finisher Edward Luke Wray was there in the 1870s and 1880s, followed by boot maker Harry Wray from the 1900s until the 1930s. From around 1920 there was an adjacent store as No. 1A that was used by offal merchant Hubert G. Hardy. Between there

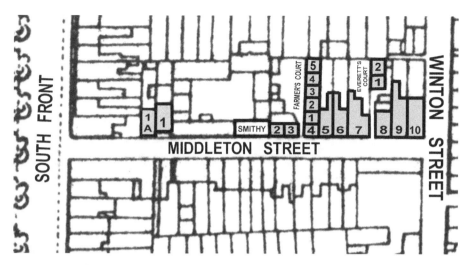

The west side of Middleton Street was a jumble of buildings and courts.

and No. 2 stood several industrial premises, including Sidney Spincer's hay and corn stores in the 1880s and, at that time, there was also a slaughter house which was operated by J. G. Boyes from 1912 to 1920. A blacksmith's shop was also there for a while.

Back in the 1850s, dairyman William Annett was living at No. 2 while carpenter Joseph Burton was there in the 1870s and 1880s. In latter years, Henry Taylor was in occupation from World War One until the final days. Joiner Philip Giles and the Glasspool family were early residents at No. 5 in the 1850s and 1860s, where Walter Fry, and later the Nash family, were occupiers from the early 1900s until demolition. No. 6 saw labourer William Penny as householder in the 1840s to the 1860s. Others came and went before the Street family spent three decades there from the early 1900s. No. 7 contained others of the Glasspool clan in the 1860s before the Rogers family had a long association there from the early 1900s until the mid-1920s.

The Hicks ladies were busy at No. 8 as far back as 1841 when Ann Hicks was a draper. Mrs Sarah Hicks was a needlewoman there in the 1850s and 1860s, long before Albert Edward Fitzsimmons and his wife became tenants from around 1912 until 1931. No. 9 saw great changes, with labourers, a laundress, a coach builder, butcher – and the inevitable boot maker – all seeing time there before William Fouch arrived in 1914 and stayed until the end.

Tinplate worker Daniel Reeves had found a home at No. 10 in 1841 and remained until the 1860s when the property became a greengrocer's shop, with John Taylor

Looking along Middleton Street Nos. 4 to 10, towards Winton Street.

there in the 1870s. It became a grocery store under Owen Errington in the 1880s and remained as such until Albert Edward Baker was the final shopkeeper in the 1930s.

MIDDLETON STREET – EAST SIDE NOS. 23 TO 11

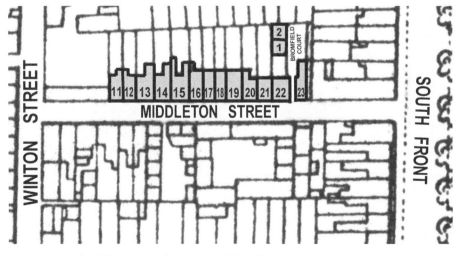

The east side of Middleton Street showing Nos. 11 to 23.

Looking north along Middleton Street towards Winton Street with Nos. 22 to 11 on the eastern side.

The houses on either side of Middleton Street were interspersed with several small courts that were not favourably reviewed in the 1893 slum report. These were:

FARMER'S COURT NOS. 1 TO 5

Farmer's Court, entered through a passage between Nos. 3 and 4 Middleton Street, had a row of five houses, each three storeys high, none of which had through-ventilation. Water was supplied through a common tap in the courtyard, which also had an uncovered ash pit and two lavatories. The houses were described as being unhealthy. Back in the 1851 census, the court was occupied by a couple of tailors, a seaman, a cook and a fly driver. A decade later we find a bricklayer, boot maker, dock labourer, baker and a jobbing gardener as there was a high turnover of occupants up until the final entry in 1914.

EVERETT'S COURT NOS. 1 AND 2

This court contained just two back-to-back houses that were accessed from between Nos. 7 and 8 Middleton Street and surrounded by high buildings. By 1893 the drains were in a serious condition, with sewage leaking into adjacent properties. The buildings were described as damp, dark and unhealthy, and having no ash pit accommodation.

In the 1861 census, the tenants were tailor Charles Wood and boot maker Edwin Parsons. The 1880s saw boot maker Frank Stainman and Robert Giles, a coal merchant's carter. Mrs Turner was resident at No. 1 from the turn of the 20th century until the house became vacant prior to demolition. William Alfred Harnett lived at No. 2 from the early 1900s until the late 1920s, when Maurice Mahoney became the final tenant at that address.

BROMFIELD COURT NOS. 1 AND 2

These were two dilapidated houses in damp and dirty condition, with a common water supply and toilets in the court, which did not contain an ash pit. Labourers Henry Hinves and John Churchill were there in 1861 and the 1880s welcomed charwoman Emily Day and fireman George Pearce. Charles Jenkins was the last of the line at No. 1 from 1912 onwards, along with neighbours the Gilroys from 1920.

The two houses that made up Bromfield Court, photographed in 1935 when Mrs K. Gilroy was living at No. 2.

WEST FRONT – PALMERSTON ROAD

Dating back to the 1830s, West Front was the western boundary of Kingsland where it ran between South Front and North Front. In more recent years it became part of Palmerston Road, which continues on from North Front to New Road. West Front was numbered 1 to 22, beginning at the *Eagle Hotel* and ending at the *Angel Inn*. Its buildings faced Palmerston Park and were substantial, with great variations in design, much like South Front. Nos. 18 to 21, which was the row between Winton (Winchester) Street and North Front, were originally known as Nos. 1 to 4 Trafalgar Place until the 1860s. Nos. 16 to 21 all disappeared, with the redevelopment of Kingsland estate, with the exception of the *Angel Inn* at No. 17, which survives.

West Front in the early 1900s looking north towards North Front with the original Eagle Hotel on the right of the photograph (Dave Marden Collection).

WEST FRONT – EAST SIDE NOS. 1 TO 11

The east side of West Front (now part of Palmerston Road) began at No. 1 the *Eagle Hotel*, which was quite different to the building that replaced it in the late 1920s. The original building on the corner of South Front dated back to the 1830s when it was called the *Joiners Arms* and the landlord was Henry Stillwell, who reigned supreme until

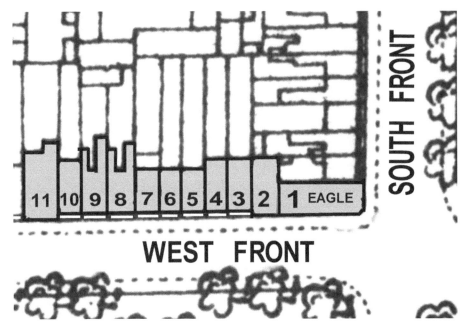

11 | 10 | 9 | 8 | 7 | 6 | 5 | 4 | 3 | 2 | 1 EAGLE

WEST FRONT

West Front from the Eagle to Nos. 10 and 11, which was also a pub, firstly the Star & Garter, then the Palmerston and finally Copperfields.

the 1860s before the pub's name was changed to the *Eagle Tavern*, then owned by Scrace's Star Brewery. Strongs of Romsey took over in the 1920s and rebuilt the pub in their mock-Tudor style. In doing so, they extended into Nos. 1 and 2 South Front and also No. 2 West Front. Another change came when Whitbread acquired the pub in 1969 and then, in 1993, converted the interior as part of their Hogshead Ale House chain. It closed in 2010 and is now a convenience store.

No. 2 had various tenants until it was swallowed up in the expansion of the rebuilt *Eagle* in the late 1920s. Likewise, No. 3 had a wide variety of residents until the arrival of Mrs Stacey in the early 1900s, who stayed until the 1920s. William Bendall at No. 4 had an even longer residence, living there from the early 1900s until the 1930s, when both Nos. 3 and 4 were replaced by Percy Hendy's garage. Hendy's also eventually took over Nos. 5 to 9, which were finally replaced by flats.

No. 5 had been the home of vocalist Henry Church during the 1880s, but by the early 1900s the premises had become a confectioner's shop run by Miss Rogers. By the outbreak of World War One, the shop had been taken over by John Moore. He and his wife continued to run it until the 1930s, when Hendy's took over the site. No. 6 was the

Nos. 10/11 Palmerston Road was originally the Star & Garter pub.

abode of several watch makers, cycle and antique dealers and No. 7 was a fancy draper's shop during the First World War and into the 1920s. No. 9 saw antique dealer Robert John Mudge trading there from the early 1900s before it became the greengrocer's shop of Herbert Harvey and his wife from the mid-1930s until the 1960s.

Nos. 10 and 11 were combined in the 1870s as the *Star & Garter* pub, belonging to the Old Shirley Brewery, before coming under the wing of Cooper's Brewery and renamed the *Palmerston* after West Front had become part of Palmerston Road. It remained as such until 1983 when Watneys re-launched it as *Copperfields*, a Dickens theme bar. It has been closed for many years now.

No. 12, through time, had been a tailor's shop for most of its early years and then a café in the 1930s and 1940s. No. 13 was a locksmith's, then also a tailor's shop but ended its days as a restaurant, in its latter days known as German Edies whose proprietor had a penchant for cutting off and collecting men's ties. No. 14 was for many years a cycle shop. Nos. 15 and 16 at one time followed the local trend and were a draper's and an antique dealer's respectively.

The upper part of West Front with Nos. 11 to 22. Nos. 18 to 21 were originally Nos. 1 to 4 Trafalgar Place. No. 17 on the corner of Winton Street was once the West Front Inn and No. 22, the Angel Inn, was previously No. 51 North Front.

Carpenter Alfred Hillier was one of the earliest tenants of No. 12 West Front and also had premises in Middle (Middleton) Street.

No. 12 Palmerston Road.

GEORGE HORNSEY,

LOCKSMITH,

𝔅ell-𝔥anger, and 𝔊as-𝔉itter,

13, West-Front, Kingsland-Place.

Glass Chandeliers, Fittings in Opal Gilt, Bronze, and Artistic, of the Newest Designs.

CONSERVATORIES, GREEN-HOUSES, PINE-PITS, &c.,
Heated with Hot Water, on the most improved principle.

MANUFACTURER OF

SHARP'S GAS COOKING APPARATUS.

The multi-talented George Hornsey resided at No. 13 West Front back in 1851 and it seems he could turn his hand to anything.

No. 13 Palmerton Road.

No. 17 was the *West Front Inn*, dating back to the 1850s, with coach maker William Thomas behind the bar. The Diddams family moved in during the 1860s and ran the pub for around half a century until handing over to Mrs Kate Bailey during World War One. She was there until the pub, owned by Scrace's Brewery, closed its doors in 1927 after its

No. 14 Palmerston Road.

licence was refused. In the 1930s it became Walter Brooker's hairdresser's shop but seems to have disappeared in the area redevelopment before the war. Back in the 1830s, No. 18 (formerly No. 1 Trafalgar Place) was the home of gentleman William Pardy, but by the 1840s it was inhabited by baker Francis Bowditch. He and his family ran the business until the 1870s. John Tizard carried on the trade through the 1850s, and by the early 1900s Edwin Cox had manned the ovens, making way for Francis Mullins in the 1920s. Mullins was the final baker when the war intervened in 1940.

No. 19 saw the Berry family at home from the 1840s to the 1870s, when brush dealer Mary Ann Sharp began her business there. John George Learmond was also selling brushes there from 1901 until the First World War, when drapers Penman & Hyslop made it their tailor's shop which ended with the outbreak of World War Two. Schoolmistress Miss S. Wilkins was in No. 20 in the 1840s and 1850s, then several other tenants followed before Mary Ann Sharp moved her brush business there in the 1880s. Willoughby Morrell was the last recorded tenant there in the 1920s. For most of its existence, No. 21 was home to the shoe-making trade. Joseph Fry and his family were cobbling there from around 1836 until the 1860s when John Kenway took up the anvil for another two decades. In the early 1900s, Benjamin Holloway continued the tradition until the 1920s when the *Angel Inn* expanded into that address.

The *Angel Inn* stood on the corner of North and West Fronts, where it once was No. 51 North Front, but from the late 1800s became No. 22 West Front. In 1869 it was owned by Welsh's Lion Brewery, but in 1920 was purchased by Fuller Smith & Turner.

The Angel Inn pub stands on the corner of what was the entrance to North Front.

It was rebuilt in 1927 and extended into No. 21. One of the early landlords was George Clench back in the 1870s. Henry Rich was in charge from the early 1900s until the 1920s. Herbert Cox then served until wartime, with William Fogerty seeing through the conflict. The pub still stands but has seen difficult times of late.

SOUTH FRONT

South Front formed the Southern Boundary of Kingsland. Running east from Palmerston Road (formerly West Front) to St Mary Street, it was part of a major thoroughfare that ran from Above Bar and through to the River Itchen. In its early days the individual houses of many designs were homes to mainly professional classes and overlooked the cricket grounds of Hoglands Park. They were all demolished by the late 1970s and replaced by blocks of flats that run along most of the former street. Originally, South Front ran through to St Mary Street and Kingsland Square but was severed in the 1960s by the Kingsway dual carriageway, which divorced it from its eastern end.

SOUTH FRONT – NORTH SIDE NOS. 1 TO 18

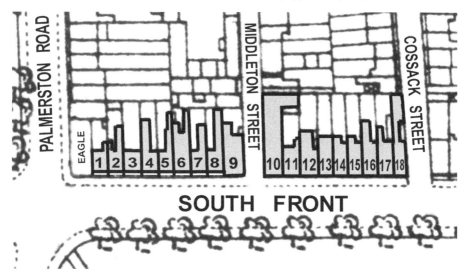

The western section of South Front in 1908 with Nos. 1 to 18 between the Eagle Hotel on the corner of Palmerston Road along to Cossack Street. No. 9 on the corner of Middleton Street was the Robert Burns pub and No. 10 was the Adelaide Hotel.

Through the 1840s, No. 1 was home to ironmonger Charles Hilton and plumber Vessey Brumfield. By the 1880s Robert Meech & Co were making bicycles there and electrician Oscar Schutze was resident from the turn of the century until the 1920s. No. 2 was the home of coach plater John Morris in the 1840s and one of the later occupants was David Davis, an interpreter for the South Western Railway back in 1887. Like No. 1, it continued as a private residence until the late 1920s when the *Eagle Hotel* was rebuilt. Miss Clark at No. 3 was a girls' school mistress back in 1839 and was followed by an assortment of tenants including reporter Walter Moody, retired innkeeper Elizabeth Stillwell and watch maker Alfred George Sheather. Mrs B. M. Baldwin was its final resident before wartime, but Harry Wilson was there in the 1950s.

The properties at Nos. 4 to 8 had all disappeared around the time of Second World War. No. 4 was the abode of pastry cook Richard Ray in the 1840s, followed by baker Edward Baachus. Then after a brief spell as a greengrocer's it became the home of Miss Maria Page, a maker of dresses and mantles. Arthur Harding was its last occupant from the turn of the century until the war broke out. R.N. Captain Bush and his wife lived at No. 5 in the 1830s and 1840s before it became a tailor's shop under Hyam Isaacs. There followed a succession of tailors until Mrs Elizabeth M. Lucas, another retired publican, was there through the 1880s. From then it remained a private residence until the end. Likewise, No. 6 had housed a mixture of fairly affluent people, including the Degee family in the 1840s and 1850s. George was a brewer and James was a retired naval officer. Antique dealer Charles Weare was in occupation from 1912 until the 1930s when it was finally a confectioner's shop under John George Butler.

No. 9 was the *Robert Burns*, a fine example of a Victorian pub built in the 1860s, which stood on the corner of Middleton Street. It belonged to the Dorchester Brewery of Eldridge Pope & Co, where George Broomfield was one of its early landlords in 1871. Gas fitter John Fry was mine host for a decade until the 1880s and this was one of the last of the old buildings to come down in the 1970s. In the 1960s, the land between the *Eagle* and the *Robert Burns* was taken up by the motor dealer Percy Hendy, whose firm became Hendy Lennox motor engineers.

On the opposite corner of Middleton Street stood the *Adelaide Hotel* at No. 10. It had been a pub since the 1850s, with William Martin being one of its early landlords through

The Robert Burns standing proudly during the early 1900s when Edgar James Gandy was landlord until the mid-1930s (Dave Marden Collection).

the 1860s and 1870s. Once owned by Crowley's Alton Brewery, it came under Watney's in 1947, who ran it until demolition came in the 1970s.

No. 11 was always a residence from the 1840s, with Frederick S. Colbourne holding the rent book from before World War One until the 1930s and a Mrs Loton living there post-World War Two until the final days. No. 12 was a rather elegant building in its day,

The substantial buildings along South Front varied in design and must have been quite desirable in their prime. Several were like this example at No. 12 that lasted for 130 years or more.

being home to florist and nurseryman James Ingram in the 1830s and 1840s. Brewer George Degee and his family, previously at No. 6, had moved there in retirement by 1871. South Front certainly had an attraction for ex-publicans as Alfred Pope, another former licensed victualler, moved in through the 1880s. By the 1930s, No. 12 had been converted to apartments, with barmaid Dora Padwick living there from the 1930s until the 1950s.

In its time, No. 13 had been home to a draper, engineer, a missionary, a salesman, and a music teacher, while at one time, back in the 1880s it had been a lodging house. In similar vein, No. 14 had been home to drapers, a ship's steward, a coach wheeler, boot maker, and latterly newsagent Ernest Scorey from the early 1900s until the late 1940s. The usual drapers and tailors were evident at No. 15 from its early days through

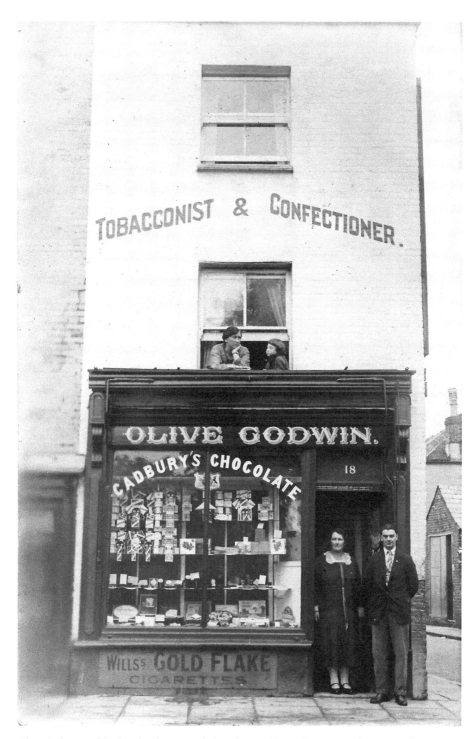

Olive Godwin and husband Sidney outside her shop at 18 South Front on the corner of Cossack Street in the 1930s (Silvia Collins).

South Front in about 1955 showing Nos. 13 to 18 with the News of the World offices on the corner of Cossack Street.

to the turn of the century, when china repairer Francis Isted was there until the 1920s saw antique dealer William Albert Mitchell set up shop there. It remained an antiques business when W. McNicol took over in the 1950s and saw out the last couple of decades there.

South Front had its usual smattering of gentleman residents in the early days, one of which was William Sutton at No. 16 in the 1840s and 1850s. Tailor Richard Diddams moved in around 1871 and had let the building out as apartments by 1884, whilst remaining there himself until 1891. Nos. 17 and 18 had the usual mixed variety of residential occupations until the *News of the World* opened its branch office at No. 17 around 1930. Until that time, No. 18, on the corner of Cossack Street, had been a confectioner's run by Mrs Olive Godwin who had taken over the shop from Cyril Nurse in the 1920s. The News office then took over the building and became a landmark in the street for many years until it was demolished with the others in the 1970s.

SOUTH FRONT – NORTH SIDE NOS. 19 TO 32

No. 19, on the other corner of Cossack Street, had its share of gentlemen in the 1840s, before welcoming the now familiar brood of tailors who seem to have congregated in the South and West Front areas in the latter 1800s. By the 1880s, Mrs Cook was running a day nursery for infants at No. 19. Absalom Pugh and his wife lived there from the early

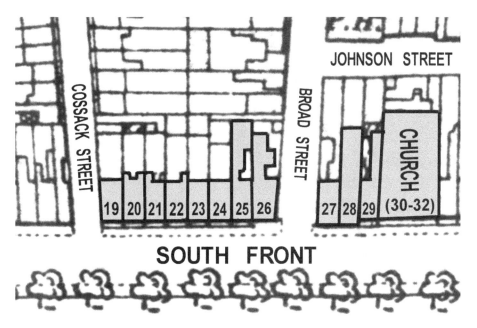

South Front from Nos. 19 to 29 with the church that replaced the earlier houses. No. 26 was the Eight Bells pub on the corner of Broad Street.

1900s until Wallace Harvey arrived in the mid-1920s and stayed as its last tenant until the 1960s. Thomas Bowman was coal merchant and ship broker, residing at No. 20 from the 1860s to 1880s. A later resident at that address was the Reverend Edward Glossop Wells, Curate of St Mary's Church. Nos. 21 to 23 all had their share of drapers and tailors through the late 1800s, with Arthur Hallum, the Holy Rood sexton, at No. 23 in the 1880s. Mrs Russell had moved in by the early 1900s and stayed until the 1930s, with Mrs Sheppard being tenant for the final two decades.

Early years at No. 24 saw carver and gilder Mark Diaper earning a living there in the 1830s to mid-1840s, when letter carrier (postman) Henry Cole moved in and remained until the mid-1850s. At one time, No. 25 was a servants' agency run by Mrs Jane Othen from the 1880s and into the early 1900s. Her husband George Thomas Othen was a local builder.

On the corner of Broad Street, at No. 26, was the *Cricketer's Arms* pub dating back to the 1850s when George Cox was beer retailer there. In fact, George was a coachman who had lived there since the late 1830s. The pub was the meeting place of the Public Land Cricket Association, very appropriate as it faced the cricket grounds in the parks

The view along South Front looking west from the Eight Bells on the corner of Broad Street (David Goddard Collection).

across the road. While leased to Panton's Wareham Brewery, its name had changed to the *Eight Bells* and a later landlord in the early 1870s was George Flood, a slater by trade, who was followed by a steady turnover of publicans. The pub was taken over by Scrace's Star Brewery in 1885 and the later arrival of mine host Harry Isaac around 1912 saw some stability as Harry then ruled the roost until the 1930s. In its final years the pub was owned by Stong & Co of Romsey, which had come under the wing of Whitbread & Co when closure came in 1971.

Plumber and glazier Jeremiah Pratt was the occupant of No. 27 from at least 1836 until 1850. It was briefly a ladies' school, run by William Newman, in the 1880s and around the turn of the century it became the shop of H. C. Taplin & Sons, who were electrical engineers. Taplins remained there almost until the end, which saw Southern Carpet Fitters as the final occupants. At No. 28 was another pub, this one named the *Lord Clyde*, which appeared in the 1860s when Collin Napier was in charge on behalf of owners Scrace's Star Brewery. The pub surrendered its licence in 1903 in favour of a new hostelry, the *St Denys Hotel*, which opened the following year in Aberdeen Road. James and Sarah Messenger had been the final hosts and Mrs Messenger stayed in residence until the mid-1920s until Arthur Richard Scorey became its final tenant before the building became a wartime bomb victim.

Looking east along South Front from the former Methodist Church towards St Mary Street in the 1950s, showing the great variety of buildings that lined its course (Dave Marden Collection).

Coachman Joseph Stevens was an early occupant of No. 29 in the 1830s, but by the 1840s it was a grocer's shop run by Charles Hill. By the 1870s it had become the abode of various bank clerks and assurance agents before William Sims saw out its final decade. Nos. 30 to 32 were occupied by drapers, tea dealers and dyers until the building of the Primitive Methodist Chapel on the site in 1884 at a cost of £3,500, which included the purchase price of the three houses. The new chapel replaced the one in St Mary Street and later was used by various other church denominations, before finally becoming Kingsland Baptist Church from 1946, which lasted until the redevelopment of the street in the 1970s.

SOUTH FRONT – NORTH SIDE NOS. 33 TO 52

The final section of South Front ran from Nos. 33 to 52, most of which were demolished in the 1960s to make way for the Kingsway dual carriageway, together with a redevelopment for flats.

No. 33 was home to architects, clerks and surveyors through the 1870s and 1880s and, from the turn of the century, all of the occupants were listed as married or single ladies. Grocer Thomas Jarvis was at No. 34 from the early 1860s to the late 1880s and, once more, most of the latter occupants were ladies. No. 35 had a variety of tenants

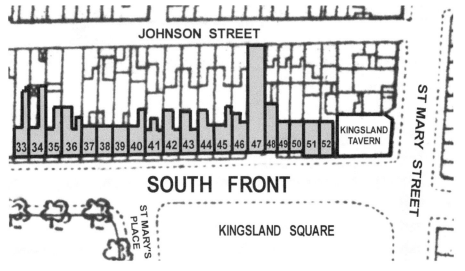

Nos. 33 to 52 at the eastern end of South Front, which at one time ran through to meet St Mary Street. The cycle works of Woodford & Farr at No. 47 extended through to Johnson Street at the rear.

in the mid-1800s, including the multi-talented William Whitcher, who was a painter, plumber and guilder around 1850. By the 1870s it had become a lodging house run by Miss Harriet King, who stayed until around 1890. Union Castle Line seaman John Cowling Rice was in residence from around 1910 to 1940.

More drapers were in evidence at No. 36 in the shape of Robert Reid during the 1840s

and 1850s, and schoolmaster William Davis Aubrey lived there from 1871 until 1907. No. 38 appears to have been one of a multi-occupancy with a wide variety of tenants over the years, with clerks, gas fitters, builders, decorators, and Mrs H. Vivian, a certified

The buildings along South Front had a wide variety of architectural designs. This was the doorway of No. 34.

nurse, during the 1920s and 1930s. No. 39 was the home of a certain Miss Mary Pingo, a woman of independent means through the 1840s. This was also the address of the Bampied family, who resided there from the early 1900s until the outbreak of World War Two. Percival Bray was the final occupant after the war.

No. 40 housed various naval personnel, including a couple of master mariners in the early days, two of whom were John and William Fuszard from the 1830s to 1850s. Later, during World War One, it was home to nurse Mrs Jane King until the mid-1930s when it became a chemist shop. During the war it was a newspaper's branch office and finally a café in 1960 when that part of the street came down. Fishmonger William Martin was an early trader at No. 41 in the 1830s, followed by the Bailey family, who were builders, and then the inevitable draper, who was Alex McQueen, resident in the early 1850s. By the 1880s, Miss Julia Barnes was running her stationery shop there before becoming a newsagent. In the early 1900s it was briefly a confectionery shop but afterwards became a private residence.

Bricklayer John Scott and his wife were in No. 42 from the 1830s until the 1860s, and after several generations of occupants it became a hairdresser's shop, with William and George Wakeford wielding the scissors through the Second World War and into the 1950s, when George Franks became its final barber. Coachman James Stone resided at No. 43 in the 1840s before tailor Richard Morgan moved in around 1850. Later incumbents included sugar refiner George Henning in the 1870s and 1880s. One other resident of note was James Heron, who lived there from World War One until the very end.

George Sims was yet another local coachman in the 1840s, this time living at No. 44 where he 'reigned' until the mid-1870s. Blacksmith Albert Avery was there through the 1880s and longer-term residents who followed were Charles Wilkins, from 1914 to 1925, and William Alfred Ede from the mid-1930s until the mid-1950s.

The Clarkson family were busy at No. 45 from the 1830s to 1850s, where James made boots and shoes, while Mrs Clarkson fashioned straw bonnets. The industrious pair had moved on by the 1870s when plumber and decorator George Bagshaw was resident through to the late 1880s. Albert Jesse White lived there from around 1912 to the 1930s, with the Farnan family being the final residents after the Second World War.

Robinsons general store stood at No. 51 South Front.

There were few occupants of note at No. 46, but No. 47 was a hive of industry with a brush maker, steam dyer and a cooper there before the address became the workshop of cycle makers Woodford & Farr from the early 1900s, whose premises extended through to No. 6 Johnson Street at the rear. Woodfords were there until the 1920s and the final occupants there were house furnishers Tom Fraser & Son. No. 48 was home to coach maker William Faichen in the 1840s and 1850s and carpenter Joseph Waterman lived there in the 1870s and 1880s. Thereafter, there seems to be several periods when the building was unoccupied until butcher George Gillett stayed for a few years prior to World War Two, after which the address looks to have disappeared from the records.

The inside of No. 49 witnessed the lives of a printer, a postman, a plumber and a cooper from the 1840s to the 1880s. By about 1930 it had become the PDSA Animal

Clinic and remained as such until after the war when wardrobe dealer Thomas Henry Medley took over the premises until that part of the street was cleared. The occupants of No. 50 were of a great variety. A book keeper, Methodist minister, bricklayer, post office clerk, watch and clock maker through the generations, and by the 1920s it had become a confectioner's shop run by Edward Thomas Hawksworth, and then G. E. Sparks through the war years until A. Corvan was the last proprietor around 1960.

No. 51 also became a shop but originally was home to a broker, carpenter, boatman, chemist and dairyman. Mrs E. A. Merriott ran it as a dairy shop from the early 1900s. At that time, the shop incorporated a telephone call office from around 1912 to 1920 when Southern Counties Dairy took over. In the mid-1930s, surgeon John Erhard Schneider lived there and by the 1950s it had become Herbert Robinson's grocery store, with Mrs G. Medley running it in the final years.

The final premises before the *Kingsland Tavern* (on the corner of St Mary Street) was No. 52 which was also a shop for most of its existence. In 1836 it was home to shopkeeper Mrs Winkworth, then baker Henry Taylor in the 1840s, and undertaker and house agent John Bisley in the 1850s. A decade later printer Arthur Spencer had moved in and opened the St Mary's Post Office there, becoming Spencer & Sons Stationers and

The junction of South Front and St Mary Street in the 1950s when the street ran past the Kingsland Tavern.

The new Kingsland estate, behind South Front, rises from the rubble of the old streets after World War Two. One or two original buildings still stand, as did the whole of South Front, which would disappear in the late 1970s (David Goddard Collection).

Post Office in the 1880s, but by the early 1900s it had changed to a tobacconist's shop, and then a confectioner's under Archibald H. Waygood throughout the First World War and continuing as such until the outbreak of World War Two. When peace returned, the premises became Lindseys surgical appliance store until the 1950s.

PART TWO – ST MARY STREET

In the early street directories, until the 1860s, St Mary Street was divided into Upper and Lower sections that were dissected by the boundary between the Trinity and St

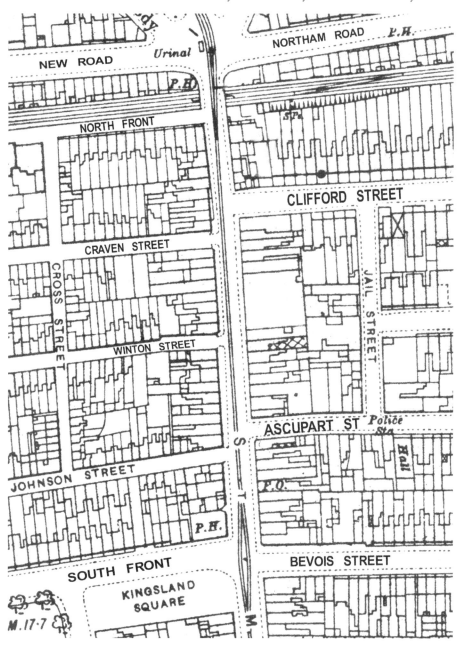

Upper St Mary Street from Six Dials down to Kingsland Square in 1908.

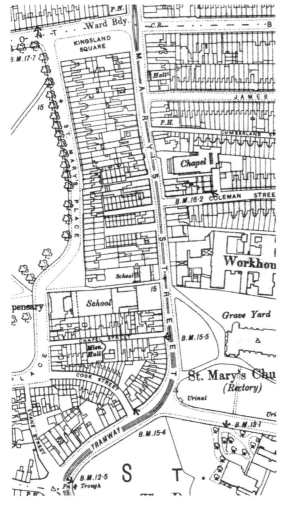

St Mary Street (Lower) from the Kingsland Square down to Evans Street as it was in 1908.

Mary's wards, which ran along South Front and Bevois Street. The Lower section was from East Street to the ward boundary at South Front and the Upper section from the boundary to Six Dials.

Today, St Mary Street retains very little of its former character and charm, with many of the original buildings having been replaced by modern counterparts, while the market is a mere echo of its former self with just a few traders who keep it ticking over. Only two of its many public houses remain and the street itself has an air of decay and neglect.

Our exploration of the past begins at the bottom of the street, where it once joined East Street. We then move north following the street numbers along its west side to Six Dials and then return south again down the east side towards St Mary's Church.

ST MARY STREET – LOWER WEST SIDE NOS. 1 TO 14

The southern end of St Mary Street in the middle 1800s was, understandably, much different from today. Back then, as shown on the 1846 Ordnance Survey map where it joined the bottom of East Street, the area was a conglomeration of tightly packed buildings, alleyways and hidden courtyards, all long since swept away. Cook Street

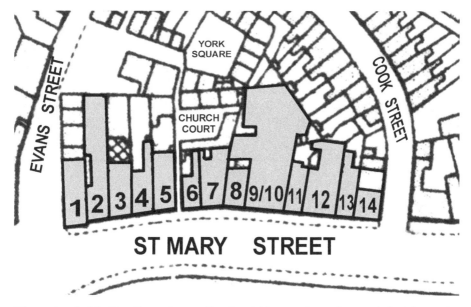

The south end of St Mary Street showing Nos. 1 to 14 between Evans Street and Cook Street. An alley between Nos. 5 and 6 led to Church Court and York Square.

still survives (if only in name) but Evans Street disappeared when the Kingsway dual carriageway was laid down from Six Dials through to Marsh Lane in the 1960s.

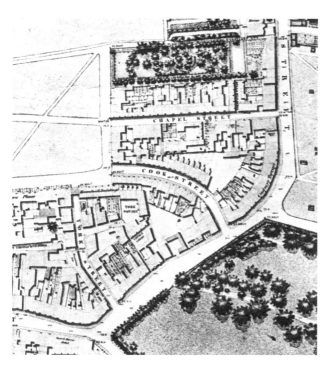

Evans Street had the earlier name of York Street and had an entrance to York Square, which, together with Church Court, could also be accessed from an

The lower part of St Mary Street between York (Evans) Street and Chapel Street where alleys led off to many packed and hidden courts. The bottom right shows the grounds of the Chantry before redevelopment that later included the Central Hall.

The lower end of St Mary Street near East Street around 1905 showing the parade of shops, Nos. 7 to 14 on the left. St Mary's church in the distance did not receive its spire until 1914.

alley named Church Row that ran from between Nos. 5 and 6 St Mary Street. The first few buildings were known as Ogle Place back in the 1840s and 1850s when baker

The opposite view of the bottom of St Mary Street in the late 1940s, where Downey's store is at the entrance to Cook Street on the right and the South Hants Motor Company on the left. The lower end of East Street can be seen behind the tram.

Eleazer Mowle was at No. 1. By the mid-1850s it had become a draper's shop and then was a grocer's shop from the 1870s, run by William R. Mitchell until the early 1900s when it became William Walton's printers. The Walton family business ran until after the Second World War when stationers Cox & Sharland moved in and, in the 1960s, No. 1 was occupied by Rentaset Radios.

Isaac Hawkins ran his pork butcher's shop at No. 2 from the early days until the late 1880s and by the early 20th century it had become home to the Premium Trading Stamp Company, but by 1912 ironmonger Herbert James Holt was there until after World War Two. E. Mayes & Sons then used the building as a store in the 1950s before Tracey's House Furnisher's occupied it in the 1960s.

No. 3 had a variety of uses. In the 1870s it was a general shop, then a cleaner's, a dining room and a fishmonger's before Holts expanded from No. 2 to occupy Nos. 3 to 5 in the early 1900s (as did Mayes and Tracey's in the 1950s and 1960s). No. 4 was the premises of whitesmith Thomas Harris in the 1840s. It afterwards belonged to a grocer, a brush maker and then a fancy goods dealer under Joseph H. Moors in the 1870s. Moors then took on several other lines such as ironmongery and china before Holts moved in. By the 1930s it was a greengrocer's and before the war it was home to Associated Automobile Supplies, who provided spare motor parts until the building was a victim of wartime bombing.

No. 5 was once Yarndley's jewellers and watch makers shop in the 1840s and 1850s, after which the Spain family set up their grocer's shop there. By 1912 it was Spencer's second-hand bookshop, which lasted until the Second World War and also fell in the bombing. At No. 6 St Mary Street was a pub named *The Green Man* belonging to Barlow's Victoria Brewery, which stood at the entrance to Church Row, and its early landlords had several side-lines. John Purse in the 1840s was also a tailor, while William Pope was a fruiterer. Henry Maskell was behind the bar from around the turn of the century until the pub was lost to wartime bombing in 1940.

At No. 7, Stephen Blundell was broker and undertaker in the 1840s and 1850s, but by the 1860s it was a dining room run by James Dacombe. From the 1870s, a number of others ran the eatery until it seems to have gone out of business in the 1920s. No. 8 was jointly occupied by corn and straw dealer Thomas Stickland and brick and tile

Nos. 2 to 5 St Mary Street with the impressive multi-premises of ironmonger H. J. Holt. To the right of No. 5 is the alleyway that led to Church Row and on the far right there is a glimpse of the Green Man pub.

man John Eckless. That combination ran until the 1860s when corn and coal merchant James Bell took over, and by the turn of the century it was Waller & Co's grocery shop. Albert Rogers ran the business from the 1920s but by 1939 Arthur Harris had turned it into an amusement arcade. After the war it was again a joint premises, in part run by C & M Distributors as an electrical accessories store, along with Melody Rentals who sold musical instruments. By the 1960s it had become a café and bar that lasted into the 1970s.

James Mandy was a clothier and shoe salesman at Nos. 9 and 10 from the early days, then William Coombes ran the address in the 1870s. A decade later, the shop had become St Mary's Coffee Tavern before being revamped as dining rooms until the 1920s, when the Dunlop Rubber Company set up their tyre business there. That lasted until the 1960s when it became Prices bakery. Coombes had also taken over No. 11 until the 1880s when James Frederick Short set up his fruit shop there. By the early 1900s Cohen & Sons had begun as furniture dealers and auctioneers, but by 1916 it had become a sweet shop run by the Anderson Family.

Back in 1847, No. 12 had been a beer shop run by Elizabeth Needham, then a furniture shop and a fishmonger's. Likewise, No. 13 had a variety of uses until the 1920s.

No. 14 was initially a grocery shop, then a hairdresser's and later a tailor's. The mid-1920s saw Nos. 10 to 14 consolidated as Downey's Drapery Store. Sydney F. Downey had previously occupied Nos. 13 and 14 and his business remained until the 1960s, which saw a change of tenancy to Liberty Coin amusement machines, while the original No. 10 became a furniture store under West Country Warehouses.

ST MARY STREET – LOWER WEST SIDE NOS. 15 TO 31

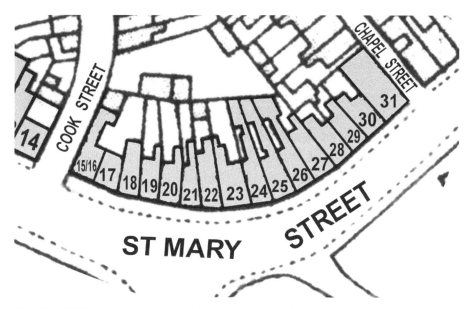

Nos. 15 to 31 between Cook Street and Chapel Street where Nos. 18 to 27 were originally named Cooksey's Terrace. Nos. 15 and 27 were both public houses at one time.

This section of the street underwent several changes over the years, particularly in the 1930s when some of the buildings were demolished and others were rebuilt. On the corner of Cook Street, at No. 15, stood another pub called the *Foresters Arms*, which appears to have gone out of business in the 1890s. It then became Frederick Dunning's boot makers shop until the 1930s when the firm of Engine Replacements Spares moved in. After World War Two the building was sub-let as Nos. 15 to 17 to several businesses such as Bells Haulage Contractors and wallpaper merchants Keeping & James.

Moving along the street, the next ten buildings opposite St Mary's Church were known as Cooksey's Terrace, named after John Henry Cooksey, a local councillor and

The building that now houses the Noodle Bar at Nos. 15 to 16 on the corner of Cook Street is the sole survivor of this Section of St Mary Street (Dave Marden).

former mayor. These were Nos. 18 to 27 (originally 1 to 10) and housed a wide variety of shops. In its time, No. 18 was once a butcher's shop and then a photographers. In 1884 it was S M & A Tyson's photography and frame shop before Thomas Lewis set up his watch making shop there around the turn of the century. No. 19 was James Clarke's boot makers in the 1840s and 1850s, then in the 1870s and 1880s it was a fishmonger's run by Richard Bowyer and his family until Thomas Lewis branched out from next door around 1900. Lewis was there until the 1920s when the two shops were taken over by leather merchants Day Brothers who were present until the 1960s. In the latter years Nos. 18 and 19 were occupied by bookmaker Fred West and antique dealer L. Rainger.

No. 20 was once a toy warehouse back in the 1850s, then Richard Bist (or Best) opened his china and glass warehouse around 1870 and, about 1912, Charles Salter opened his butcher's shop there until poultry dealer Charles Wilkins took over through the 1930s. From the 1950s, horse slaughterers Passey & Sons were present until around 1970. The Passey family had previously run their businesses at No. 100 near Six Dials. In latter years No. 20 became Mitch's hairdresser's and then Connor & Mitchell's sports shop.

THE OLD ST. MARY'S
PORTRAIT SHOP.

Cartes de Visite, 4s. per Dozen.

"WHY PAY MORE?"
GEMS, 12 for 9d.

S. M. & A. TYSON,
PICTURE FRAME MAKERS, GILDERS, PHOTO-GRAPHERS, & PICTURE DEALERS.

A large assortment of Mouldings always kept in Stock. Wholesale and Retail.

GOOD WORK AT LOW PRICES.

OLD FRAMES RE-GILT EQUAL TO NEW.

18, ST. MARY STREET,
(Opposite Chapel Road),
SOUTHAMPTON.

Tyson's photography shop at No. 18 offered a wide variety of services back in the 1880s.

Cabinet maker Charles Malvern ran an upholstery and paper-hanging business at No. 21 in the 1840s and 1850s. It then became a butcher's shop, dining room and china shop until saddler Alfred James Walker opened his leather shop there around 1900, a business that lasted until at least the 1970s. No. 22 was variously a baker's and a butcher's in the early days but by 1901 had become a tobacconist's run by Frederick Lewis until the mid-1930s when the building was demolished. The same fate awaited No. 23 that was a chemist's shop run by William Alfred Clark since the 1920s. In fact, it had always been a chemist's since the 1840s under Thomas Valentine, and later with Richard Primmer and then John Bienvenu behind the counter from the 1850s and through the 1880s.

No. 24 had been a bakery until Mrs A. M. Aitchenson opened her fancy draper's shop there around 1900. Then in the 1920s it became Rose Fudge's ladies' and babies' outfitter's. This was another building demolished in the 1930s. No. 25 lasted a little longer before falling to wartime bombs. Watchmaker Henry Tapley had been there since the turn of the century but it had been a furniture shop before then. No. 26 was a butcher's shop for most of its existence, under various ownerships since the 1850s. Before that it had been a leather shop and a bookseller's.

No. 27 was another building that was once a pub. Having previously been a grocer's shop, it was taken over by boot and shoe maker John Penton in the 1850s and named the *Stag*, but within a decade it had been renamed the *Netherbury Arms*. It went out of business in the 1890s and became a hosiery shop run by William James Fudge, which lasted until the wartime bombing destroyed the building.

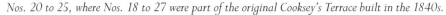

Nos. 20 to 25, where Nos. 18 to 27 were part of the original Cooksey's Terrace built in the 1840s.

Nos. 28 to 31 back in the 1930s with the entrance to Chapel Street on the right, showing Robert Judd's newsagents, Leonard Wheeler's barber shop and Thomas Metcalf's general store. There is a glimpse of No. 27 that had once been a pub called the Netherbury Arms.

Nos. 20 to 27 were rebuilt in the 1950s and occupied by fireplace specialists Summers & Co, while No. 28 became the Reema Trading Company along with the sale makers W & T Avery.

No. 28 was latterly Robert Judd's newsagent's shop, but from the 1840s it was the abode of the Purse family, who made straw hats and bonnets through to the 1870s when John Purse continued trading there as a tailor until the mid-1880s. In its time, No. 29 had been a boot maker's shop, a greengrocer's and a sewing machine shop until the turn of the century when William Kellaway opened up as a hairdresser there and remained until the 1930s when Leonard Wheeler took up the scissors. Thomas Metcalf ran a general store at No. 30, prior to which the premises had been an outlet for fancy goods, fish, fruit and bicycles.

No. 31 had also been a cycle shop for many years run by John Alfred Eyers. It was originally a baker's shop in the 1840s to 1870s. George Eliot was the last proprietor there as a dealer in animals.

ST MARY STREET – LOWER WEST SIDE NOS. 32 TO 47 (LATER NOS. 36 TO 47)

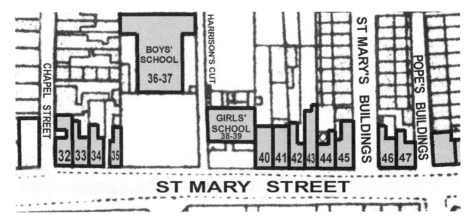

Nos. 32 to 47 showing the boys' and girls' schools either side of Harrison's Cut, that were associated with the workhouse on the opposite side of the street.

The buildings between Chapel Street and Popes Buildings were Nos. 32 to 47. The old workhouse schools (Nos. 36 to 39) had gone in the 1920s, leaving a gap in the numbering, and Nos. 32 to 35 were demolished in the mid-1930s. This section was later renumbered 36 to 39 when being rebuilt after the war.

No. 32, on the corner of Chapel Street, was always a pub dating back to the 1840s and named the *Eagle Tavern,* then renamed *Eagle Inn* from around 1900. It was owned by Crowley's Alton Brewery and had a bad reputation for drunkenness, finally being closed in 1921 after being described as a disorderly house. Herbert Hayter was the final landlord and afterwards he and his wife Ida ran a pet shop business there, but by the late 1930s the business had moved further up the street to No. 67.

No. 33 was the home of Henry Bromley, a wood turner who was also a sexton at St Mary's Church. He lived there from the 1840s to the 1880s. Boot Maker Edward Candy was there at the turn of the century before confectioners Edward and Jane Smith moved in and stayed until the building came down. No. 34 was another pub that fell victim to the mid-1930s demolition of the area. From the 1870s, this was the *Prince Consort* that had once been a boot maker's shop and then an eating house back in the 1860s. It was leased to Panton's Wareham Brewery but was taken over by Scrace's Star Brewery in 1892 and finally belonged to Strong's of Romsey in its final days.

TRAMWAYS.

NOTICE.

BANK HOLIDAY

AUGUST 1st, 1898, the

OMNIBUSES

THROUGH

ST. MARY'S

Will run from 8 a.m. every 20 minutes till 12 noon and every 10 minutes thereafter to and from the COMMON and ITCHEN BRIDGE.

LAST 'BUS FROM COMMON - - - - 10 P.M.
LAST 'BUS FROM ITCHEN BRIDGE - 10.28 P.M.

Universal Fare - 2^{D.}

The Bitterne and Hampton Park 'Buses will run at usual times.

Universal Fare (for this service) - 2^{D.}

BY ORDER.

Before the electric tram arrived in St Mary's, there was an omnibus service operated by the Corporation Tramways Company. On August Bank Holiday in 1898 a flat fare of 2d was in place all day. The Itchen Bridge mentioned was, in fact, the floating bridge.

Herbert Hayter with one of his specimens in the doorway of the Eagle Tavern. He later moved his menagerie up the street to No. 67.

No. 35 had been a shop since the 1850s, in its time being a greengrocer's, a general store and a tailor's. By the 1880s, William Pothercary had set up his fruit store there, which remained a family business until the end.

Harrison's Cut, running between St Mary Street and Houndwell, is still evident but much changed these days. At its entrance, fronting on to St Mary Street, was the home of one John Butler Harrison in the 1830s and 1840s. He was holder of many civic offices in the town and was related by marriage to novelist Jane Austen who, on her visits to Southampton, would possibly have stayed there. At the rear of the house, on both sides of the cut were tree-lined gardens. Upon Harrison's death in 1850, the house and gardens were sold off, the land being developed for boys' and girls' schools attached to the Workhouse opposite in St Mary Street. One can only imagine the classes of children from poor families would have represented something like those featured by Dickens in *Oliver Twist*. Schoolmaster Frederick Willcox and Mistress Mrs Harland presided over the children in its early days and the schools were demolished in the 1920s.

Nos. 40 and 41, since the early 1900s, had been Charles Edward Moody's hosiery shop until around 1930 when it became Moody & Co's outfitter's and overalls suppliers, which remained until fairly recent times. Many will recall the advertisement on the side of the building featuring a workman in his overalls being hoisted by a crane. In the past,

Moody's outfitter's shop at Nos. 40 and 41 was resident alongside Harrison's Cut for many generations.

No. 40 had been a tailor's since the 1860s and then Harris's second-hand clothes shop in the 1870s and 1880s. Until Moody moved in, No. 41 had previously been William Budden's bookbinding and stationer's shop through the 1850s to 1880s.

At No. 42, Mrs Martha Lovell and her daughter Eliza were dressmaker's and milliner's in the 1840s and 1850s. By the 1870s it had become an ironmonger's and then a fried fish shop from the early 1900s until the 1930s. During the war it was Arthur Hampton's sweet shop (who also moved into No. 43) and by the 1950s it had become A & B Utilities hardware shop, later reverting to an ironmonger's and tool shop.

In its early days No. 43 was a hairdresser's in the 1840s and possibly a beer house named the *Shipwrights Arms*, but certainly by the 1870s it had become the *Resolution Inn*, belonging to the Winchester Brewery and later to Fuller, Smith & Turner of Chiswick. It was refused a licence in 1907 and became Hampton's sweet shop until after the Second World War. In the 1950s it was taken over by A & B Utilities hardware, who also had the shop next door at No. 42.

The Mason's Arms at No. 45 is another of St Mary Street's lost pubs. It still stands but is now converted to flats. Next door at No. 44 stands another St Mary Street original building. In more recent years it was the well-known Pantry Cafe (Dave Marden).

Looking east from St Mary's Buildings towards St Mary Street, as the locals pose for the camera in about 1930. The original Masons Arms pub can be seen on the right (Courtesy of Gary Hampton).

No. 44 was for many generations the Pantry Café. Back in the 1840s it was a grocer's shop run by pilot Charles Marsh until the 1860s when it became, briefly, Thomas Hammond's butcher's shop, an outfitter's, and then a picture-frame maker's. From the early 1900s it belonged to a succession of wardrobe dealers until becoming a café after World War Two.

On the corner of St Mary's Buildings, the *Mason's Arms* at No. 45 was once a butcher's shop until it became a pub in the 1860s. In the early 1900s it was run by Albert Walter Crook, who also ran a fishmonger's at No. 46. He gave up the pub in the mid-1920s in favour of Albert Dominy, who remained in charge until at least the 1950s. The pub had belonged to Barlow's Victoria Brewery and latterly Brickwoods, Whitbread and finally Gales of Horndean. It closed in 1994 and has now been converted to flats.

Nos. 46 and 47 were a pair of isolated buildings that stood between St Mary's Buildings and Popes Buildings. No. 46 was firstly a grocer's shop back in the 1840s but later in the decade it was that of several beer retailers. By the 1850s it was a greengrocer's run by the Burridge family and remained as such until the mid-1870s when it became a

Lower St Mary Street in the early 1900s looking north with Nos. 40 to 45 on the left and the railings of the workhouse on the right (Dave Marden Collection).

fishmonger's under James Rogers. Albert Walter Crook had taken over the business in the early 1900s while doubling as mine host at the *Masons Arms* on the opposite corner until the 1920s.

Cabinet maker James Bryer was resident at No. 47 in the 1840s and 1850s. It then became a draper's and a boot maker's before being converted to a butcher's shop in the mid-1880s. W & R Fletcher ran the business from the early 1900s until the 1920s when George Wolstenholme began building prams there. A decade later, Archibald Martin was making picture frames there until after the war when Crook's Fishmonger's expanded from next door, remaining as Crook's Fishmongers until well into the 1970s.

ST MARY STREET – LOWER WEST SIDE NOS. 48 TO 60

There were five businesses between Popes Buildings and Coronation Terrace numbered 48 to 52. No. 48 was always a butcher's shop stretching back to the 1840s when Charles Powell was in charge, while No. 49 in its early days was a beer shop managed by John Harris, who was also a cooper by trade. It was then a tailor's, boot maker's, a hairdresser's, greengrocer's, and a watch maker's in the 1870s and 1880s. In the early 1900s it was

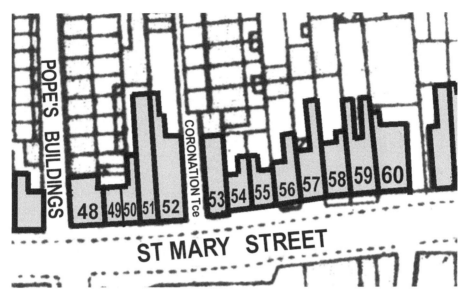

Nos. 48 to 60 on the west side of St Mary Street where Popes Buildings and Coronation Terrace have long since disappeared.

once again a hairdresser's then a greengrocer's in the 1930s before returning to a barber shop after the war. In more modern times it was Armstong's Health Food shop.

No. 50 was yet another beer house back in the 1840s, run by one Joseph Judas LeDain. Sawyer Charles Dawkins presided over the pumps around 1850 until it became a pork butcher's until the mid-1870s when a succession of uses included the sale of paint and wallpaper, fruit, photography, second-hand books and sewing machines. By the 1920s it had become a sweetshop run by George Grimes until after the war. It remained as such under several owners, being the Candy Shop in latter years. No. 51 was a baker's shop, with Charles William Fellows at the oven in the 1840s and early 1850s. Then came a succession of bakers until, under Robert Hills, it became a herbalist shop selling surgical goods until more modern times in the 1970s.

Last in the row was No. 52, which was mostly a draper's boot and shoe warehouse in its time, which was run by Russell & Sons from the 1930s until the 1960s. By 1970 it had become Stoner's motor accessories shop. No. 53 was yet another beer house back in the 1840s, which afterwards became a greengrocer's by the 1860s. By the early 1900s it was a fishmonger's and then a butcher's and, for many years after the Second World War, was Hampton's Confectioner's before becoming Hingston's antique shop in the 1960s.

The aptly named Thomas Trim was at No. 54. He had been cutting hair since the 1840s, with his son William taking over the scissors in the 1870s and 1880s. By the turn of the century it had become a butcher's shop and then Mrs A. Harris's dining rooms before the First World War, and by the 1930s George Glanville had set up his poultry business there. From the 1950s it had become Anderson's chemist shop through to the 1970s and the building was later taken over by expansion of the *Oddfellows Arms* next door. No. 55 appears in the directories as a greengrocer's shop or fruiterer's from the 1870s, but there is no mention after 1930 when it became part of the rebuilt *Oddfellows Arms*, which further extended into No. 54 in more recent years.

No. 56 was once a pub named the *Blacksmith's Arms* back in the 1840s. By 1880 it had become the *Pilot Inn* but by 1871 it had been renamed the *Oddfellows Arms*, run by William Goff for Forder's Hampton brewery. Courage's took over the pub in 1923 and rebuilt it in the 1930s when it was extended to take over Nos. 55 and 54. The pub ceased trading in 2008 afterwards being demolished and replaced by a block of flats.

For over 60 years, No. 57 was a draper's shop from way back in the 1840s, but by 1912 the Keats family had set up their grocery shop there, which lasted until Leslie

Original buildings at Nos. 57 to 61 have survived in the modern era and their use has changed with the times (Dave Marden).

James Walker took over the business in the 1930s. After the war it was Hampton's Confectioner's until the Surplus Trading Company moved in during the 1960s. No. 58 was another draper's shop until umbrella maker George Beaman arrived around 1912. Howard Joseph Jones took over the umbrella business in the mid-1930s then, after the war, it was briefly Fudge's outfitter's and then a florist in the 1950s before the TV rental company D.E.R. was there in the 1960s and 1970s.

Timber merchant George Brown was at No. 59 from the 1830s to 1850s, when shoe maker Charles Sheppard set up the family business there in the 1860s and remained until around the turn of the century when it became a tailor's shop and then a bazaar run by William George Cook before the outbreak of World War One. In peacetime it became a furniture shop and then R W L Delbridges corn merchants from around 1930, when Henry Hawthorn-Hill set up a dentistry above the shop after moving there from No. 67. Hill practised there until the start of the war and was the grandfather of Southampton comedian Benny Hill, whose real name was Alfred Hawthorn-Hill. Delbridge's were still there in the 1960s, as was the dentistry which had changed hands several times since the Second World War.

No. 60 was James Arnold's greengrocery shop in the 1840s and 1850s, but by the 1880s it had become a tailor's shop and then a sweet shop for most of the early 1900s. Delbridges expanded from No. 59 next door after the war, and then a couple of furniture businesses took over both buildings from the late 1960s.

ST MARY STREET – LOWER WEST SIDE NOS. 61 TO 74

No. 61 belonged to a couple of umbrella makers before becoming a leather merchant's and then a confectioner's around 1910 when William H. Woodger moved in. By the 1920s he was also a newsagent until Saul S. Cohen took over prior to the war. A further expansion by Delbridge's saw them move into both Nos. 61 and 62 after the war, and, as they were already resident at No 59 from the early 1900s, they now occupied Nos. 59 to 62 consecutively. After Delbridge's moved out in the 1960s, Nos. 61 and 62 became a bookshop and an electrical contractors respectively.

Butcher and corn dealer Charles Clear was at No. 63 from the 1830s until about 1850, after which various corn dealers were there until it became a grocery shop in

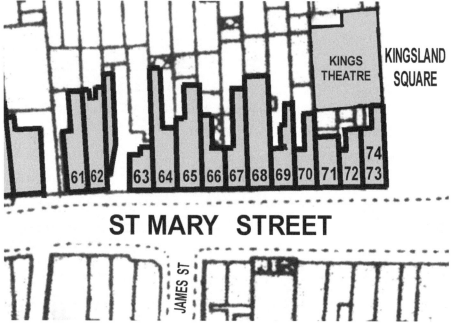

Nos. 61 to 74 St Mary Street contained no less than three pubs at Nos. 68, 70 and 73 in close proximity to the market on Kingsland Square. The Kings Theatre faced the square from 1914 until destroyed by bombing in 1940.

the 1870s. Another change came around 1912 when it became J. M. Millett & Sons draper's, but by 1916 Robert Joseph Selby was making false teeth there. He had gone by the 1920s when it was briefly a milliner's before the mid-1930s saw Speedwells Shoe Repairs set up and remain until the 1960s.

No. 64 was originally a lodging house run by Mrs Attwood, but it soon became a tailor and draper's shop. By 1870 Robert Enos Harris had begun his bakery and confectionery business there until around 1912 when James Giles Payne continued the role. By the mid-1920s it had once again become a tailor's shop under Alfred Haysom, who was in situ until the late 1950s when it became Wilson & Legg's china and glass dealers.

The Emery family had a long-standing bakery and grocery business at No. 65 from the 1830s until the 1850s. It continued as such under various others until the 1880s. By the new century it had become a furniture shop and then the Singer sewing machine shop from the mid-1920s. After the war it became a café, for many years run by Joseph Barnett, and by the 1970s it was a florist.

No. 66 was yet another grocer's shop and briefly another draper's until the 1870s saw carver and guilder William Summers set up his picture-framing works there. Joseph Harvey continued the service in the early 1900s until another aptly named firm of Taylor & Son set up their tailor's shop which lasted until after the Second World War, when the long standing butcher Ernest Albert Chard moved in and his name remained over the shop until at least the 1970s.

As far back as the 1830s, Mrs Charlotte Hedges was a shopkeeper at No. 67 and by the 1850s she and her daughters ran a toy warehouse there. In the 1860s, George Westcott and his wife had moved in. He was a builder and she ran the shop as a general dealer. By the early 1900s it was a tobacconist's, for many years run by Harry Edwards then, before the outbreak of World War Two, pet shop owner Mrs Ida Hayter had moved there from the former *Eagle Tavern* at No. 32 in the late 1930s. Hayter's pet shop became well established and ran for many years until that part of the street was rebuilt. The tiny shop was alive with bird cages and the walls were festooned with every type of cage accessories and millet sprays.

No. 68 was a butcher's shop back in the 1830s, but by 1871 it was a pub named the *Bold Forester* run by James Housten, which belonged to the Winchester Brewery. It closed in 1928 and then became a tobacconist's shop run by the Copson Family until about 1970 when it became the Cards and Candies gift shop. Unlike most of the properties in St Mary Street, No. 69 saw only a couple of businesses for most of its time. Boot maker John Bishop set up his shop there in the 1840s and the successful family business lasted until about 1914 when outfitter Lewis Price took over and remained until at least the 1970s.

Schoolmaster William Dawkins was at No. 70 during the 1830s and 1840s, then afterwards it was a marine stores until Martha Brinsden opened the *Oddfellow Inn* there in about 1870 (not to be confused with the *Oddfellows Arms* at No. 56) under the Old Shirley Brewery. In 1888 it was taken over by Complin's Cobden Bridge Brewery and then sold to Fullers from 1898. By 1903 it had been renamed the *Chiswick Arms*. A further change came in 1903 when it came under Brickwoods and the name was changed yet again in 1909, this time to the *Arundel Castle*. The pub closed in 1928, with William G. Bennett being the final landlord. Coincidentally, it then became a Florist's shop run by William S. Bennett and Bennett's Florist blossomed there until the 1970s.

Back in the 1830s, No. 71 began as a pork butcher's under Joseph Oakley, who ran the business until the 1850s when it became Clark's Marine Stores. By the early 1900s it was William White's hairdressers until Bennett's took it over for a short period in the 1930s. Just before the war it became Price & Sons pie shop until the 1950s when it changed to Complin's bakery. In the 1960s it was a delicatessen but by the 1970s it had become Delbridge's pet store.

No. 72 was a hairdresser's, then a boot makers during the 1840s, where the Gilbert footwear business ran until the 1880s. By the early 1900s it was a pork butcher's that was taken over by Edward Albert Chard prior to World War One. William King moved in prior to the Second World War and it remained a butcher's shop until the 1950s saw it changed to John Francis jewellers, remaining as such until the 1970s when it became an oriental food store.

Isaac Madge's tailor's shop stood at No. 73 in the street's early days, but by 1871 it had become Mrs Esther Bragg's second-hand clothes shop. By the turn of the century, J N Brown & Co had set up a boot makers there which lasted until the mid-1930s when the *Plume of Feathers* pub next door was rebuilt and extended.

Lots of activity in the Kingsland Market area. This photograph dates from the late 1800s before the trams came to St Mary Street. The service there didn't begin until 1901 (Dave Marden Collection).

Looking north up the street past Kingsland Market in the early 1900s. Interesting to note that not much had changed by the time of the following photo (Dave Marden Collection).

Another view up St Mary Street towards Kingsland Market in the late 1940s where there was a fine collection of shops. On the left are No. 65 Joseph Barnett's Café, No. 66 Chard's butcher's, 67 Hayter's pet shop, 68 Copson's tobacconist's, 69 Lewis Price outfitter's, 70 Bennett's florist, 71 Prices pie shop, 72 Kings butcher's and 73/4 the 'Plume of Feathers' pub (Dave Marden Collection).

The Plume of Feathers pub on the corner of Kingsland Market in the 1970s which closed in recent years and has now become a Buddhist Centre (Dave Marden Collection).

The *Plume of Feathers* at No. 74 was yet another of St Mary Street's old pubs dating back to the 1850s. Belonging to Panton's Wareham Brewery, it was taken over by Scrace's Star Brewery in 1892 and later by Strongs of Romsey, who demolished and replaced the original building in the 1930s, at the same time taking over the former No. 73 next door. The pub ceased trading in 2011 and is now a Buddhist centre.

Behind the Plume of Feathers was a yard (No. 75) used by coach builder James Henry Higgs in the 1880s and was later Walter Olive's stables in the early 1900s. By 1914 the site was occupied by the Kings Theatre, otherwise known as the Kingsland Picture House. Facing onto Kingsland Square, many of its patrons would dally after the Saturday evening performances to pick up bargains from the market as it closed. The Kings provided entertainment for the local population until being destroyed by wartime bombing in 1940. Its ruins stood neglected until finally cleared away in 1955.

Kingsland Square has been a market place for generations and flourished in the 1880s. A steady decline began in the mid 20th century, which was accelerated by the building of the Kingsway dual carriageway in the 1960s. In the 1980s the City Council sought to revamp it by replacing the ramshackle timber and canvas stalls with unified

The Kings Theatre facing the Kingsland Square in the 1930s. It had provided entertainment from 1914 until destroyed by bombing in 1940 (Dave Marden Collection).

counters and canopies under an all-covering roof. As such, it was a failure as traders and customers complained about the dismal darkness under the roof, which had destroyed much of the market's character. The roof was removed and the market now survives in a much smaller form but with very few traders in recent years.

Kingsland Market at its peak in the 1930s with the Kings Theatre on the left and the buildings of South Front to the right (Dave Marden Collection).

In the old days of costermongers, barrows were allowed on the Kingsland Market square. Tom Hampton (left) and his brother-in-law Ted Cresswell worked their pitch in the 1920s. South Front forms the background (Photo courtesy of Gary Hampton).

ST MARY STREET – UPPER WEST SIDE NOS. 76 TO 85

The west side of St Mary Street with Nos. 76 to 85 from the Kingsland Tavern to Winton Street.

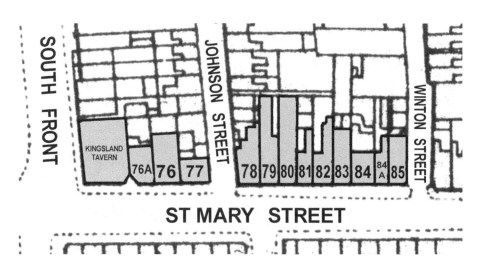

Upper St Mary Street looking north from the Kingsland Tavern seen on the left of this postcard from the early 1900s. The former music hall and public library at No. 76 is the tall building next door (Dave Marden Collection).

The section of the street northwards from South Front was known as Upper St Mary Street, it being north of the ward boundary between Trinity and St Mary's wards. The *Kingsland Tavern* stands facing the market place. At one time, before the building of the Kingsway dual carriageway in the 1960s, South Front ran through to St Mary Street. Sometimes listed as No. 76, the *Kingsland Tavern* dates back to the 1820s and was once owned by Forder's Hampton Court Brewery but was taken over by Brickwoods in 1925 and remains as one of only two pubs surviving in St Mary Street. Back in the 1840s it was run by William Haysom, who was also a coach proprietor, and Frederick Bartholomew was a long-standing licensee through the Second World War until the 1950s.

The building next door is also listed as No. 76. These days it is known as St Mary's Sports Hall but it has an interesting history. At one time it was the site of the tap bar of the *Kingsland Tavern*, with adjacent stables and outbuildings. Back in the 1840s it was run by Mrs Elizabeth Pugh and a number of fly proprietors kept their carriages there. By 1884 it had become a Masonic Lodge but a new building was soon erected on the site, which by 1887 had become a music hall known as The St Mary's Hall of Varieties. By 1889 the building was housing Southampton's first public library, which moved to

Looking across the Kingsland Square towards the Kingsland Tavern in the early 1900s where South Front still meets St Mary Street. Across the road we can see Hart & Co's house furnishers at Nos. 124 and 125, Rueben Hallum's undertakers at No. 126 and Baker & Co's outfitter's at Nos. 127 and 128 on the corner of Bevois Street (Peter Wardall Collection).

Thomas Nicol was licensee of the Kingsland Tavern around the turn of the century and this photo shows him with a pony and trap outside his pub on May Day 1898 (Dave Marden Collection).

The former music hall, library, mission and sports club at No. 76 St Mary Street where once stood the tap bar for the tavern next door – and then a Masonic hall. A newsagents and grocery shop then occupied part of the ground floor (Dave Marden).

London Road in 1893. In later years it became the Hercules School of Physical Culture and, by the early 1900s, was the Southampton Holiness Mission and Church of the Nazarine. Various ground floor parts of the building have been divided over the years to house a newsagent's shop and a grocer's, for many years run by Archibald Cecil Winter, more recently as A. C. Winter & Sons.

No. 77 was once George Oliver's boot and shoe warehouse from the early 1900s until the 1930s, then a pram maker's shop run by Mrs Maude Redstone prior to the Second World War, after which it became general dealers run by Thomas Stephenson and later William Stephenson's Wardrobe shop. In more recent years it became Johnnies Fishery and is still a fishmonger's today.

On the corner of Johnson Street, No. 78, was the *Dorsetshire Arms* pub, going back to the 1840s when the Paddick family ran the place for 40 years or so. It belonged to Aldridge's Bedford Brewery when Mrs Annie Loveday was behind the bar from the early

The impressive features of the Dorsetshire Arms at the turn of the century on the corner of Johnson Street. It survived for over 130 years until closure but the building still stands.

1900s until the 1930s, but by the time it closed in 1974 it had become a Brickwoods house and was then finally belonged to Whitbread. Afterwards, it had something of a revival as the Clan Scotland Club and then became a sandwich bar.

The Edmunds family ran a bakery at No. 79 in the 1850s but a decade later it was a grocer's shop. By the turn of the century it had become Tubb & Sons furniture dealers. Then, from World War One it was Gerard's butcher's and remained as such until the 1970s. Tailor John White cut his cloth at No. 80 in the 1850s before moving into the furniture business in the 1860s. Next door, rivals Tubb & Sons took over the shop in the early 1900s before it became Bricknell & Co's confectionery in 1914. They were there until the outbreak of World War Two, after which the shop went back into the furniture business under Wards Distinctive Furnishings and then was Tracey's House furnishers by the 1950s. In latter years it was the Rumbelows television rental store and then an Asian fashion house.

Upper St Mary Street looking north towards Six Dials from the Dorsetshire Arms pub on the left. This photo, taken in the mid-1960s, shows the street in its final successful period with its original buildings still intact. However, big changes were on the horizon.

No. 81 had an equally checkered history, beginning as James Pollard's carpentry shop in the 1840s. By the 1850s, as Pollard & Son, he went into making cane chairs. Charles Hardiman had opened his draper's shop there in the 1870s and 1880s. In the early 1900s, Edwin Mouncher was conducting his undertakers business there until hosier and hatter James Compton moved in around 1914. From the 1930s it became Eathornes outfitter's until the Second World War. In peacetime it was taken up by Groves Electrical Engineers and in the 1960s was Leadales outfitter's before the fast-food fad welcomed Kentucky Fried Chicken there in the 1970s.

Midwife Maria Barrow lived at No. 82 in the 1840s and 1850s, an address shared with John Saunders who was a master at the British School. In the mid-1850s, George Davis had set up his boot shop there, but in the early 1870s it was a beer house run by James Read before becoming dining rooms under George Whitfield. In 1876 the building was listed as the *Marquis of Lorne*, which is likely to have been the name of the earlier pub. By the early 1900s until the 1930s, the eatery was being run by William Henry Staples, and then by the Moody family until the war. After the war it became an outfitter's under the names of H. Leadale & Company and Vogue of London.

John Burridge ran his greengrocer's shop at No. 83 in the 1850s, but a decade later George Thomas Tubb had set up his furniture shop there. Tubb & Sons were still there in the early 1900s when fruiterers Locksheath Nurseries moved in, after which there was a succession of greengrocer's through the 1920s. In the 1930s it became a provisioner's under Louis Rogers. After the war it was briefly L. Athey's barber shop until horse meat dealer Allan Hodgeson opened a butcher's shop there. Hodgeson & Son were there until the 1970s and Wilkins the Baker's occupied part of the premises in the 1960s and early 1970s.

Brush maker Thomas Thompson occupied No. 84 back in 1845, but two years later furniture broker John Russell had taken over the address, along with next door, which was numbered 84½. He and Isaac Russell ran the business until the 1860 when Mrs Trott became a fancy goods dealer there, but that venture was short lived when No. 84 became a pork butcher's shop and No. 84½ was let to boot and shoe maker James J. Wallis. The butcher's shop ran from the mid-1880s until the 1960s under Thomas Ponsford & Son, while 84½ became a draper's shop under Moses Millett in the early 1900s and was then W. Egerton & Son's fishmongers from World War One until Charles Knott took over the business in the late 1940s. By the 1960s the two properties had

Misselbrook's grocery shop at No. 85 St Mary Street on the corner of Winchester (later Winton) Street about 1890.

merged into one under grocer's Kelsall & Drew. Then in the 1970s it had become the Curry Centre Indian Restaurant.

In its early days No. 85 was a beer house run by the Shutler Family in 1845, and afterwards by several other landlords. By 1863 it had become a greengrocer's run by Charles Edward Smith and then from the 1880s a grocer's run by Frederick Misselbrook, later known as Misselbrook & Weston until the 1960s. In the 1970s it became a bakery run by S. B. Lowman & Sons.

ST MARY STREET – UPPER WEST SIDE NOS. 86 TO 102

Dairyman Alfred Ireland was at No. 86 on the corner of Winton Street in the 1840s, but by the 1850s it had become a butcher's shop run by the Hammond family, which lasted into the 1870s. By the early 1900s it had been taken over by the International Meat Company, but by the 1920s it had become James Henry Harley's watch-making business. Harley was previously further up the street and stayed at No. 86 until the 1960s, but by the 1970s the building had become a snack bar.

No. 87 was the home of school mistress Miss Eliza Pittard through the 1840s and 1850s. By the 1860s it had briefly become a pork butcher's, before Cornelius Snook set up his fruit and vegetable shop there in the 1860s. By the early 1900s it had become a Home & Colonial store, which lasted until the 1970s when Liptons took over.

Gentleman John Leach resided at No. 88 in the 1840s and undertaker John Bondfield was there in the 1870s, but by the turn of the century it had become another of the

The top of St Mary Street's west side between Winton Street and Six Dials. Nos. 100 to 102 on the corner of North Front saw many changes and additions over the years, with the shops over the railway arriving in the late 1930s.

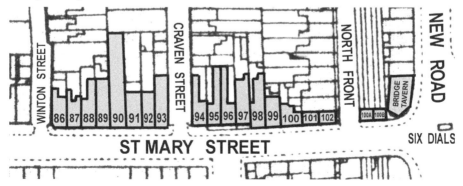

The Snook family ran several shops in Southampton. This one at No. 89 St Mary Street belonged to Richard Snook.

street's many butcher's shops. W. & R. Fletcher ran the business until the 1920s, while the British & Argentinean Meat Company was there in the 1930s. Butchers C. Kingston were then long-serving occupants through to the 1970s when Liptons extended from No. 87 next door.

Painter George Oxwith lived at No. 89 in the late 1840s until the premises were taken over by boot maker William Soper through the 1850s and 1860s. From the 1870s it was a fishmonger's until the 1880s, but from the early 1900s it was the Snook family's greengrocery shop before Liptons moved in during the 1920s. They were there until the 1970s when butcher's Dewhurst took over.

No. 90 saw several professional persons in residence from the 1840s until the 1880s, including language teacher Edmund Charles Lawless, schoolmaster Charles Welch, photographer George Southgate and band master David Crook. In 1884 it was a piano and music warehouse run by James F. Sharp, after which it belonged to the Victoria Bazaar Company in the early 1900s, when Henry James Bosley took over. He ran the bazaar but in the 1920s he became a general dealer before moving into the bicycle trade during the war. Bosley, who had been a radio engineer since the 1930s, was there until the 1960s when he dabbled with television aerials. He also had a shop across the road

Bosleys Bicycle shop at No. 90 in the 1960s also did a line in television aerials. BBC2 on 625 lines had just arrived.

at No. 102. No. 90 was latterly a bookmaker's shop before that part of the street was rebuilt.

The *North Star* pub was at No. 91, dating back to 1851 when Alfred Ireland was in charge. William and Sarah Crumley had taken over in the 1870s under Welch's Hyde Abbey Brewery and later under Cooper's Brewery in the 1900s. A serious fire there occurred in 1989 and two years elapsed until it reopened, but its time as a pub ended as a Watney House when that section of the street was demolished and rebuilt a few years later. My own recollection of this pub tells me it was very small. The front public bar had seats that were no more than shelves along the wall and, at the weekends, a partition was thrown open to the back lounge and patrons could enjoy the added comfort for a penny or two extra on their drinks.

For part of its early days, No. 92 was a tailor's shop, but by the 1860s had become established as a booksellers where James Frederick Sharp also offered a carving and gilding service in the 1870s. By the 1920s it had become David Carmichael's fruit

The back lounge bar at the North Star was only usually opened at the weekends or on special occasions.

shop, and after the war it was yet another of the streets many butcher's shops under several ownerships until fast-food arrived in the 1970s when it was the Bake 'n' Take and afterwards a Chinese takeaway named Chefs.

Back in the 1830s and 1840s, the Langford family lived at what became No. 93. James Langford began brewing there in the 1840s and by the 1850s it had become established as the *White Swan* pub. Its name had then changed to the *Black Swan* by 1853 and it was run by the Smith family from the 1880s until the 1920s. It had been the property of Scrace's Star Brewery until its closure in December 1923. The premises, on the corner of Craven Street, was then taken over by druggist Maurice Edwin Tidbury, whose chemist shop remained there until at least the 1970s.

Standing on the other corner of Craven Street at No. 94 was another pub, this one being the *Red Rover*, named after the stage coach that ran between Southampton and London. In the 1870s Mary Ann Herford was both baker and beer retailer there. By the 1880s James Henry Hallom was running it as a beer house and general shop. Owned by Forder's Hampton Court Brewery, it was refused a licence in 1913 and was taken over by boot makers Henry Eburn and his wife Maud. They were there until the 1930s when outfitters Wood & Son moved in. At that time, Maud Eburn moved next door to No. 95

and ran a leather shop. No. 94 then seems to have been empty for a while until furrier Leon Brady was there in the 1950s, followed by decorator and wallpaper merchants J. H. & W. Reynolds in the 1960s. House furnishers Forfar & Company had the premises in the 1970s.

The 1870s and 1880s saw Ann Stacey in residence at No. 95, then in the early 1900s, Harry Applin sold hats there until hosiers Henry Chard & Co took over prior to World War One. By 1916 Henry James Bosley was running his bazaar there (Bosley also had spells at Nos. 90 and 102) until the 1930s saw Maud Eburn move in from No. 94. Maud was there until the 1960s when John Adams Bookservice arrived and remained until the 1970s, when Forfar & Company extended their furniture business from No. 94.

Baker John May had been at No. 96 since the 1830s and was working his ovens until the 1860s. It was also home to school mistress Mary Ann Pearce, who lived there through the 1840s and early 1850s. Carpenter John Hewitt was there from the 1850s until the 1880s, when shipwright Mark Symons and his wife moved in. Mrs Symons occupied her time by cleaning feathers. In the years leading up to World War One, Boots Cash Chemist's were at that address, but by 1916 boot maker Henry James Morgan was plying his trade there. Smarts Cooked Meats were in occupation briefly in 1931 and butcher William King had taken over before the war. King's butcher's shop was then long established and still there in the 1970s.

Plumber and painter John Oakley was householder at No. 97 from the 1830s until the 1870s. where his wife was a straw bonnet maker. By the mid-1870s dealer James Beavis had set up his china-and-glass warehouse there, which ran until the mid-1880s. In the early 1900s it was a dairy run by Francis William Godfrey but that was short lived when butchers James Nelson & Sons took over prior to World War One. After that war ended, Charles Knott and his son established a fishmonger's there which ran until the 1960s. Charles became something of an entrepreneur in buying the Banister Estate and establishing a speedway and greyhound stadium, and also a skating rink there. No. 97 then had a complete transformation as Darina's ladies' hairdresser's, which continued into the 1970s.

Nos. 98 to 100 were originally Nos. 1 to 3 Albany Place. At what became No. 98, cow keeper and dairyman James Gravett sold his milk there from the 1830s until the 1860s. It was then a furniture shop, clock makers and a fruiterers through the 1870s and

1880s. In the early 1900s it was a fishmonger's before becoming George Greenwood's bakery by 1912. Bakers A. J. Snook and Champions were there in the 1960s until antique dealer F. J. Hillier ran the shop in the 1970s.

Drapers Renwick & Crosbie were at No. 99 in the 1850s. Gas fitter and bell hanger William Stillwell lived there in the 1870s until Henry Charles Wooldridge opened his pork butcher's shop there in the 1880s. Wooldridge continued trading until the 1920s when Alfred Roles took over the business and he and his sons were there until the 1960s. By the 1970s it had become Son's fish & chips café.

No. 100 was the residence of gentleman George Hinves through the 1830s and 1840s when Robert Stannard moved in and ran a grocery business there for a short while. By the 1860s, Edward Donkin was making boots and shoes there. The Southampton Drug Company were operating there in the 1880s but early in the 1900s the shop became a tobacconist's run by William James Pitt and it remained Pitt's tobacco shop until the 1970s, when J. Attwool took over the business.

The building on the corner of North Front and St Mary Street was originally No. 1 North Front. At some time around 1880 it was divided into two shops which became

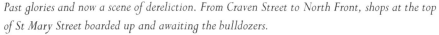

Past glories and now a scene of dereliction. From Craven Street to North Front, shops at the top of St Mary Street boarded up and awaiting the bulldozers.

Nos. 101 and 102 St Mary Street. In the 1930s, 101 became No. 100A and 102 became 100B. Around that time, a new building was erected over the railway line against the bridge, which was referred to simply as St Mary's Bridge. When Nos. 100A & 100B were demolished the new building then took their numbers. All very confusing, and a similar palaver occurred on the opposite side of the street.

The original No. 101 (later No. 100A) was White's boot warehouse in the 1880s. Burrow & Son continued the boot business in the early 1900s until Liptons ran their tea and provisions store there from 1914. The Maxim Machine Company made prams there in the 1920s and 1930s and Millets Draper's were there in 1935. Then, in the war years, it became Michael George Bedwell's furniture store. After the war, Bolloms Dry Cleaner's moved in until around 1960, when J. E. Mansbridge opened up his carpet shop. Kingsland Carpets took over the business in the 1960s and 1970s. It was later Speedwell shoe-repair shop.

In the 1880s the original No. 102 (later 100B) was where Frederick Allen combined his talents for window-blind making and selling tobacco and, for a short while, Henry Shrimpton ran his newsagents there. Watch maker Henry Harley was established

The shops above the railway line at the top of St Mary Street where the Shirt King was best known. The former Bridge Tavern pub behind is located in New Road.

Devastation at the top of St Mary Street as a World War Two bomb destroys buildings around the railway bridge at the north end. The entrance to North Front is at the centre of the photo (Dave Marden Collection).

from the early 1900s until around 1920. It became a sweet shop by the 1930s, where Maynards were in residence until the 1960s when it was reinvented as Ross's Snack Bar, which remained into the 1970s.

An interesting view looking south from Six Dials at the top of St Mary Street in the early 1900s. On the left is No. 2 Northam Road, which was lost in the war and never rebuilt. On the right is the Bridge Tavern and just beyond, over the railway bridge, is Henry Harley's watchmaker's shop.

A later post-war view of St Mary Street looking south from Six Dials with a little greenery on either side of the junction.

In the 1930s a new building appeared at the top of the street between North Front and The Bridge Tavern. It was built against the west side of the railway bridge and above the railway line. Originally, it was two shops but was most famously later known as

Not strictly St Mary Street, but the Six Dials area at its junction with Northam Road was a busy place. For some reason a group of lads have gathered at the entrance to the underground toilets there (Peter Wardall Collection).

the Shirt King. The new shops became Nos. 100A and 100B after those with the earlier original numbers had been demolished. The early traders there were A. E. Kent's biscuit store (100A) and Finlay & Co tobacconist's (100B). Furrier Leon Brady was in 100A through the war years and into the 1950s. Outfitter's Siegler Clothing (trading as the Shirt King) arrived and took over both shops around 1960 and were there until the 1970s.

ST MARY STREET – UPPER EAST SIDE NOS. 101 TO 119

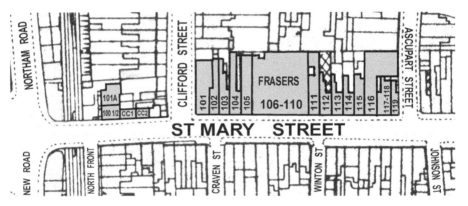

The top end of St Mary Street's east side showing the two Clifford Cottages (CC1 and CC2), the first of which was the Turners Arms pub until closure in 1913 and demolition. Four new buildings were erected afterwards as Nos. 101C, 101D, 101E and 101F. No. 119 on the corner of Ascupart Street was once the Alton Tavern.

The top of St Mary Street's east side between the railway bridge and Clifford Street saw several changes and another numerical palaver. Back in the 1870s there were three properties, with the first being numbered 100½, which housed two businesses, and the other two were known as Clifford Cottages. No. 100½ was shared by a hairdresser's and a sweetshop. George Guest was a turner by trade and did some hairdressing on the side back in the early 1870s. George G. Faulkener took up the scissors from the mid-1870s while Henry Bull and his wife ran their confectionery business next door.

Clifford Cottage No. 1 was the home of George Cavell, who was also a turner by trade, and by the 1870s the address was the *Turners Arms*, a pub being run by his wife. The pub belonged to Scrace's Star Brewery and had several landlords over the years, the last being Mrs Annie Binstead when it closed in 1913. Cottage No. 2 was a private residence and looks to have disappeared at the same time as the pub closure.

The Turner's Arms at No. 1 Clifford Cottages at the top of St Mary Street. It was in business from the 1870s until 1913 (Phil Warren Collection).

In 1916 No. 100½ was still home to Henry Bull's confectionery shop, but by then he had been joined by Tom Wendes, who ran a cats' meat business. Certainly by the 1920s, the whole group of buildings had been replaced by four new properties numbered 100C, 100D, 100E and 100F. 100C was Lloyds Bank, 100D was the cats' meat shop, by then taken over by Edward Passey, the confectionery shop, now 100E was in the hands of C. G. King and 100F was the Midland Bank on the corner of Clifford Street.

100C remained a bank until at least the 1970s and has since been a night club and a restaurant. 100D changed hands after the war when Edward Passey moved down the street to No. 20. It was later a chemist's shop in the 1960s and a tile dealers in the 1970s. 100E stayed as a sweet shop until the chemist next door extended there in the 1950s and afterwards the two shops were taken over by the tile dealer Pacemaker Tiling. The Midland Bank was still in operation at No. 100F until it became the Golden Nugget amusement arcade in the 1970s. These days the building is used by the city council.

No. 101 on the south corner of Clifford Street was a corn merchants back in the 1870s, but by the 1930s it had become a grocery store and remained so until after the war when Zona's outfitter's moved in. By the 1960s, along with No. 102, it had

Staff gathered outside the Maypole Dairy shop in the early 1900s. Maypole were at No. 104 until the 1960s.

become the premises of A. E. Russell and Sons who, apart from selling shoes, issued cheques for credit shopping. In the meantime, No. 102 had been variously a grocer's shop, piano warehouse, and a saddlers, before H. J. Bosley & Co moved in during the 1920s. They were general dealers before becoming radio engineers in the late 1930s. By the 1960s they had moved across the road to No. 90 where, by the 1960s, they were selling bicycles and TV aerials.

Walter Austen had opened his chemist's shop at No. 103 around 1871 and the business became Boots Cash Chemist's during World War One. Boots were there until the 1970s, when John Adams Bookservice moved in.

George Ivemy set up his tailor's shop at No. 104 in the early 1860s and by the 1880s he had been joined by his brother Charles, who was already established in the trade. The early 1900s saw the shop become the Maypole Dairy, which it stayed until taken over by

Frasers Department store occupied Nos. 106 to 113 in the 1960s. On the far left of the photograph is Sydney Man's shop and Boots the Chemist.

menswear suppliers Sydney Man's shop in the 1960s. Sydney's also moved into No. 105, which had been a pawnbroker's shop since around 1870. From the turn of the century until the 1950s it was run by Josiah Hollis.

No. 106 was a butcher's shop run by George Hawkins in the 1860s, but it had become a draper's shop by the 1880s under William Thomas Smith. Tom Fraser took over the business with his son prior to World War One, expanding into Nos. 107 to 110. By the 1970s the store had become Marley Homecare. Isaac Russell was a furniture dealer at No. 111 in 1863 and his family continued the business, also at No. 112, until the 1960s when Frasers department store took over until it became Budgen's Supermarket in the 1970s. Frasers had also moved into No. 113 by the 1930s.

Edmund Rogers was in No. 114, where he ran his grocery business back in the 1870s. A succession of grocers ran the shop until it was taken over by the Co-op from the 1950s until the 1960s. Afterwards, it was June Webb's ladies outfitter's in the 1970s.

No. 115 was a pub named the *Burton Ale House* dating from the 1870s, belonging to Scrace's Star Brewery. However, it was refused a licence back in 1928 and evolved as a furniture store run by William Joseph Hill until it became S.P.Q.R furnisher's after the war until the 1950s when the Co-op expanded from next door. Edward Neale's lead

Tram No. 78 came a cropper after being derailed and ending up on the pavement near Chard's butcher's shop at No. 66 in 1947. Frasers department store is on the right (Dave Marden Collection).

Barriers are erected around the derelict and partially collapsed No. 119 on 31 August 2018 (Steve Marden).

and glass works were at No. 116 and extended into Ascupart Street back in the 1880s. Neale's were there until 1959 when the shop became Henry's Records. Henry's was originally opened at No. 136 by Henry Sansom in 1956, but as business flourished he then moved to No. 116 in May 1959. After many years of success the shop closed in 1988 and Henry spent his retirement in Dorset, where he died aged 70 in 1993. William Lewis set up his jewellery business at Nos. 117 and 118 in the 1880s. With his son, the family business remained until taken over by D. R. Hurrell in the 1960s.

No. 119, on the corner of Ascupart Street, was once the *Mechanic's Arms*, back in the 1860s, but in the 1871 census it was called the *Pear Drop Inn*. By 1880 it had become the *Alton Ale House* and the *Alton Tavern* a decade later. Belonging to Crowley's Alton Brewery, it was refused a licence in 1928 and later became a greengrocer's shop, run by Cornelius Charles Clark and later under Clark Brothers. In recent years the building had fallen into a derelict state and partially collapsed on 31 August 2018, with the site being cleared soon afterwards.

ST MARY STREET – UPPER EAST SIDE NOS. 120 TO 128

William Lampard set up his baker's shop at No. 120 on the corner of Ascupart Street as far back as the 1860s. The family business ran until it was taken over by John Henry

Nos. 120 to 128 between Ascupart Street and Bevois Street.

WEDDING CAKES!   WEDDING CAKES!

FOR THE LARGEST SELECTION IN THE TOWN GO TO

<u>J. H. BIGLAND</u>, 120, St. Mary Street,

Buns, plain and fancy Cakes, and pastry of every description.

NEW TEA ROOM NOW OPEN—MOST MODERATE CHARGES. VAN delivers to all parts of the Town
NOTE THE ADDRESS—VICTORIA STEAM BAKERY, 120, ST. MARY STREET.

An advertisement for Bigland's Bakery extolling their range of cakes and pastries in times gone by.

Bigland around the turn of the century and, despite a few changes of ownership, the shop remains as Bigland's Bakery to this day. At No. 121 Richard Snook ran a greengrocery business for several decades from the early 1880s. By the 1950s it had become a fruiterer run by the Baker family, which lasted until the 1960s when it became a fish and chip shop called The Venture.

No. 122 has had a very mixed past. It was a drapery back in 1871 then became a chemist's shop in the 1880s, at one time run by Frank G. Racine, before becoming a tailor's shop during the First World War. It then became a tobacconist's, a butcher's, and a wine merchant's. After the Second World War it was an electrical accessories store under the name of Progress Cables until it reverted once again to a butcher's shop under T. E. Phillips & Sons in the mid-1960s.

Bigland's shop at No. 120 on the corner of Ascupart Street. It has been a baker's since the 1860s and has survived through several ownerships (David Goddard Collection).

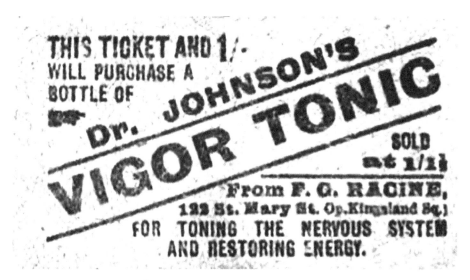

A penny ha'penny discount if you purchased Dr Johnson's Tonic with a one shilling ticket from Frank Racine's chemist's shop at No. 123.

At No. 123, John Beeston was a tailor and furniture dealer in the 1860s. By the 1870s he had become a tailor and undertaker, and his funeral business continued there until the 1960s when the shop became R. Baker's fruiterers. The Beeston company is still very much evident today, although now part of one of the major funeral companies.

No. 123A was a stationery shop from the 1880s before it became a Post Office under John Luckham in the 1880s. He was there until the 1950s and St Mary's Post Office continued until recent years saw it move into the local Tesco Store.

Alfred Hallum ran his saddlery business from No. 124 back in the 1860s until the 1880s. The shop became a furniture dealer's in the early 1900s until the 1920s. In more recent times it became a bakery and then Atlantic Dry Cleaner's & Launderette in the 1960s, along with an extension into No. 125, which was at one time a fishmonger's between the two world wars. In the 1860s, undertaker Stephen Blundell had set up his business in No. 126. Rueben Hallum took over in the 1880s and the firm of R. Hallum & Son followed, which still exists today, although it has long since ceased to be a family business. It is now run by Co-op Funeralcare.

Thomas Major was a grocer at No. 127 from around 1870 until outfitter Baker & Co had moved in around the turn of the century. But that was short lived as Nos. 127 and 128 became the house furnisher's of William Martin, which lasted until the 1920s when

John Beeston had been at No. 123 since the 1860s and was originally a tailor. His undertaker's shop was there until the 1960s.

The buildings at Nos. 126 to 128 on the corner of what was Bevois Street – Now Jonas Nichol Square – are a few survivors along that part of the street. The superstore has been many things in its time, including a chemist's, butcher's, outfitter's, house furnisher's, tailor's, radio shop and a wallpaper store (Dave Marden).

John Bright set up his gent's tailor's shop there. After World War Two, No. 127 became a café and radio dealers and J. & M. Stone moved into No. 128 around 1960. No. 128A was a collection point for the Locksheath Laundry before the Second World War, after which it became an upholsterer's run by Henry Maunder. Then, by 1960, it had become Joseph Harrisons hairdressers shop'

ST MARY STREET – LOWER EAST SIDE NOS. 129 TO 141

This section along the east side of Lower St Mary Street ran from No. 129, on the corner of Bevois Street, down to the Workhouse at No. 154. No. 129 was another of those buildings whose use changed many times over the years. It was James Stranger's grocery shop in the 1870s before Major & Co took over in the 1880s. In the early 1900s it was a piano warehouse run by Henry Price Hodges and by the 1920s it was a baker's shop run by D. H. Beak until the war. In peace time it became Jock's Café for a few years, then continued under several owners before becoming Mannings Chinese Restaurant

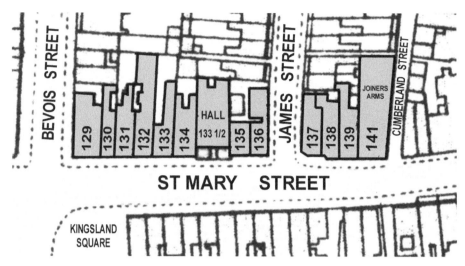

Nos. 129 to 141 between Bevois Street and the Joiners Arms on the corner of Cumberland Street. No. 140 seems to have disappeared in the late 1800s.

in the 1960s. The name later changed to the Cherry Blossom restaurant and it is now a betting shop.

No. 130 was a draper's shop in the 1850s, run by James Bailey, but by the early 1860s it had become Charles Hooper's pawnbroker's, a family business that lasted there until the outbreak of World War Two. Afterwards, general dealer D. P. Mills moved in, then, in the 1960s, it became a grocery shop run by F. Baker. No. 131 was once a newsagent's and tobacconist's, run by James Charles Cox in the 1850s. Hairdresser Henry Stroud had taken over by the 1870s and the shop remained a barbers until the turn of the century when it was briefly a cycle shop for Woodford & Farr. Boot maker Walter Bonner plied his trade there until the 1920s. There does not appear to be much more activity until Joyce Parkes opened her ladies' outfitter's there in 1950s. In the 1960s it was J. Mills bookshop and afterwards a Ladbrokes betting shop.

As long ago as the 1840s No. 132 was a pub called the *Unicorn*, run by Henry Grant. It was owned by Aldridges Bedford Brewery until it closed in 1927. John Alford was its final landlord, who had been in charge since the 1880s. After closure it had several uses until it became John Maxwell's Outfitter's in the 1950s, and then the Tumble-In café in the 1970s.

The records show that back in the 1830s James Wheeler ran a baker's and confectionery shop at No. 133. By the mid-1840s it was run by William Pledger, who

Celebrations by the staff of Beaks bakery shop at No. 129 on the corner of Bevois Street back in the 1930s, possibly for the coronation of King George VI in 1937. Hoopers pawnbroker's shop at No. 130 is on the right.

Tram No. 25 rattles south down St Mary Street past Nos. 130 and No. 131, which was Walter Bonner's boot shop in earlier days (Dave Marden Collection).

The Unicorn pub at No. 132 closed in 1927. Back in 1905, here it stands between Woodford & Farr's cycle shop and the Walpole herbal store, run by H. Rowe with its dentist's surgery above (Dave Marden Collection).

was there until the mid-1850s. In the 1870s it was still a baker's shop run by William Lenny. Then, after a brief spell as a tobacconist's in the 1880s, pastry cook Henry Moody moved in. In the early 1900s it became a herbal remedy store run by A. H. Rowe before emerging as The Walpole, herbal remedy and dental stores, where W. Aloysius Browne made false teeth. The Walpole closed in the 1930s and in the early years of the Second World War it was an amusement arcade run by Mrs A. Harris. Following a brief spell as a bookshop after the war, then a foot clinic and a one-day cleaner's before its later days as a betting shop.

At No. 134 William James Bracher ran a lead-and-glass warehouse in the 1880s and by the early 1900s this had become the Singer Sewing Machine Centre, but around the outbreak of World War One The Walpole owner and teeth maker W. Aloysius Browne had expanded from No. 133 where they traded until the 1950s. It then became the premises of wine merchants Gibbs Mew & Co.

A glimpse of old St Mary Street around 1905 looking south across from the Kingsland Square towards James Street, where Nos. 130 to 136 include Hooper's pawnshop, Woodford & Farr's cycle store, The Unicorn pub, Rowe's (Walpole) herbal remedy shop, the Oddfellows Hall, Longman's machine shop and Peckham's bakery (Dave Marden Collection).

A similar view taken in 1957 when the street was still smart and prosperous.

The view today shows most of these original buildings, dating from around 1840, are still standing, although their businesses have changed considerably (Dave Marden).

St Mary's Primitive Methodist Chapel was founded by baker James Wheeler, who traded at No. 133 in the 1830s and 1840s. Over the years, the chapel was numbered as 133½. A replacement church had been built at South Front in the 1880s and the

A look back in the opposite direction with Walpole's store, the Unicorn pub and Woodford & Farr's cycle shop on the right (Peter Wardall Collection).

The Walpole Botanic Dispensary at Nos. 133 and 134 produced herbal remedies for a multitude of ailments.

St Mary's building was then used by the Oddfellows as a meeting hall and social club until 1966, after which it has had several uses such as an auction room and a night club.

John James Jeffrey was a blacksmith and ironmonger at No. 135 around 1850 and, in 1871, Mrs Jeffrey was running a pram maker and smith shop at that address. Coppersmith Ambrose Butler and his wife Maria had taken over the

The Primitive Methodist Chapel sometimes listed as No. 133½ as it appeared in 1900 after becoming the Oddfellows Hall.

May 1910 saw a parade marking the Oddfellows centenary with the procession making its way down St Mary Street to the Oddfellows Hall.

Henry Sansom outside his record shop at Nos. 135 and 136 St Mary Street in the late 1950s. By 1959 he had moved to larger premises at No. 116.

business by 1876 until at least the late 1880s. Albert Longman was a domestic machinery dealer there in the early 1900s, before making way for furniture dealers William Edward Rayner and his wife by 1912. Following World War One, the shop became a tea room, a florist and then a hairdresser's run by William Frederick White, who was there until World War Two.

After the war Nos. 135 and 136 became Webbers Restaurant. In 1956 Henry Sansom opened his record store at Nos. 135 and 136 and became something of a legend in the street. By 1959 he had moved to new premises in a busier part of the street at No. 119 (which see). The shop was then taken over by Hartex the Printers in the 1960s. In latter years, No. 135 became a bookmaker's and the venue of the Mermaid Club and the Captain's Cabin Club. In its earlier years, No. 136 was William Peckham's baker's shop from the 1880s until the 1930s when Louis R. Bedford took over the business until Webbers moved in.

Mrs Mary McLean ran a grocer's shop at No. 137 on the corner of James Street from the 1830s until about 1850. The address was shared with builder John Whitcher and

A personal appearance by singer Frankie Vaughan in the late 1950s was enough to attract a fair crowd outside Henry's Record Shop at Nos. 135 and 136 on the corner of James Street. The building on the left is the Oddfellows Hall.

The interior of No. 135 to 136 in its time as the Captain's Cabin Club during the 1970s.

later with tailor Henry Haysom. By the 1860s it had become the pork butcher's shop of William Staples until another change of use transformed it into the store of second-hand furniture dealer William Mudge in the 1880s.

Next door, at No. 138, was the firm of Edward Strange and John Barnard, who were painters, plumbers and glaziers based there in the 1840s and 1850s. After a series of changes, which saw William Pavey as boot maker there in the 1880s, Nos. 137 and 138 were combined to become the Public Benefit Boot Company in the early 1900s. They were later known as Lennards, who remained until the mid-1920s when the Walpamur paint company moved in. The mid-1930s saw another change when the Surplus Clothing Company took over until the 1950s, when clothier Edlas began a long tenancy that lasted for several decades.

Mrs Ellyet was a seminary at No. 139 in 1853, but a decade later that was the baker's shop of Robert Harris until boot maker William Pavey took over for the next 20 years or so. Millet & Sons the draper's were there briefly in the early 1900s before it became a confectioners before the First World War. Thomas Hedge ran the shop from then and the family business continued to around 1960. No. 140 housed plasterer George Bone and Stonemason Richard Grant through the 1870s and 1880s, but it seems that address was vacant afterwards and had disappeared by the turn of the century.

A segment of lower St Mary Street looking south from James Street showing Nos. 137 to 153. Many of these are the original buildings (Dave Marden).

No. 139 standing between the Edlas clothing store and the Joiners Arms was at one time a baker's, a draper's, and then a sweetshop for much of the 20th century.

The Joiners Arms Hotel in its original splendour of Victorian craftsmanship. On the right is Cumberland Street.

The *Joiners Arms* stood, and still does, at No. 141 on the corner of Cumberland Street. Dating from the 1850s, it is now one of only two of St Mary Street's pubs that still survive today. It was purchased from the owners by Eldridge Pope & Co back in 1883 and is these days a popular music venue.

ST MARY STREET – LOWER EAST SIDE NOS. 142 TO 154

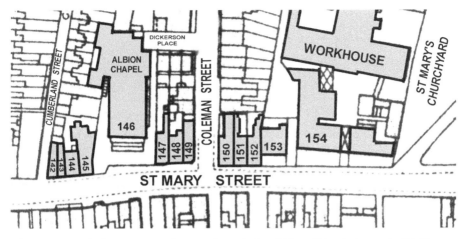

The southern end of St Mary Street's east side, with Nos. 142 to 154, which was the Workhouse adjacent to St Mary's Church.

Under the old numbering system, Joseph Bull was listed at No. 32, near the corner of Cumberland Street, and his neighbour William Cossens (otherwise Cozens or Cousins) was next door at No. 33. Their premises were either on the site of, or behind, what became Nos. 142 to 143 and the pair had set up as building and surveying firm Bull & Coussens in 1832, Bull being a carpenter and Cossens a bricklayer and plasterer with a large timber yard and sawmill between James Street and Cumberland Street. The partnership lasted until 1852, following which Joseph Bull & Sons became one of the most prolific builders in the area, working on many projects for the town, the South Western Railway Company, and the local Gas Company. There are too many others to list but they included churches, railway stations, banks, the town gaol in Ascupart Street, and the new workhouse north of St Mary's church. At one time they were employing 600 men.

No. 142 became a butcher's shop back in the 1850s with Henry Wingham in charge until the 1870s. Hairdresser George Dyett snipped away at No. 143 in the 1840s but by the 1870s it was a greengrocer's shop and then a tobacconist's. By the 1880s it was a draper's run by Henry Hawkey. Thomas Turner opened his butcher's shop there in the early 1900s and by the 1920s William Thomas Ayling had expanded his own butcher's business from No. 142 next door, and from that point the two premises became one.

Since then it continued as such until around 1930 when E. Brown & Son arrived. They were the last butchers there, remaining until the 1950s. After that, the address became a DER television rental shop in the 1960s and 1970s.

No. 144 was, in its earliest days in the 1840s and 1850s, a grocer's shop, and remained so until the 1880s when Henry Hawkey expanded his draper's shop from No. 143 next door. By the early 1900s it had become James C. Conroy's ironmonger's, who also occupied the premises next door at No. 145 for a while. Shoecraft boot repairers had moved into No. 144 at the outbreak of World War Two, but by 1960 the shop had become the premises of Wessex Typewriter repairs.

At one time in the 1830s and 1840s, No. 145 had been a police station manned by officer William Gosney. It was afterwards a grocer's shop in the 1880s until Conroy's Ironmonger's moved in. After the war, butchers F. Phillips & Sons took over and further changes came around 1960 when No. 145 became the National Provincial Bank (later Natwest). Both premises were still trading in the 1970s until both the buildings, and the accommodation above them, were later turned into flats.

Nos. 142 and 143 behind the car were once combined as a butcher's shop while the larger building as Nos. 144 and 145 had a variety of uses over the years. No. 144 was, at times, a grocer's, draper's, ironmonger's and a shoe repair shop. No. 145 was once a police station, butcher's and a bank (Dave Marden).

ALBION CHAPEL
ST. MARY'S STREET,
SOUTHAMPTON,
(LATE THE SOUTH HANTS INFIRMARY).

THE ABOVE

CONGREGATIONAL CHAPEL
WILL BE
OPENED
FOR PUBLIC WORSHIP,
On Lord's Day, September 15th, 1844,
WHEN
TWO SERMONS
WILL BE PREACHED.

That in the Morning, at a Quarter before Eleven, by the

REV. DR. ALLIOTT,
OF YORK ROAD CHAPEL, LONDON,

And that in the Evening, at Half-past Six, by the

REV. T. ADKINS.

Collections will be made to liquidate the Debt incurred by the purchase and alteration of the Building.

SUNDAY SCHOOL
WILL BE COMMENCED ON THE SAME DAY, AT NINE O'CLOCK A.M.

FLETCHER AND CO., PRINTERS, SOUTHAMPTON.

A poster for the opening of the Albion Chapel in 1844.

In 1843 a Wesleyan Tabernacle stood at what became No. 146, and by 1844 it had become the Albion Congregational Chapel, and stayed as such until services ceased in 1935. After the war it was known as the Albion Hall and occupied by Elson's Transport, who ran a removals and storage business. Downer

The Albion Congregational Chapel was founded in the 1840s and served its worshippers until 1935. Its later use was as a removals and storage depot before demolition in the 1970s.

Baker Transport had taken over by 1960 and were the final occupants before the building was demolished in the 1970s.

Joseph Tucker's china warehouse occupied No. 147 in the 1850s. It had been a tailor's shop in the 1870s, but by the 1880s it had become the premises of furniture broker Edward Tolfree. Harry Robinson opened his draper's shop there in the early 1900s and by the First World War it was George Goodacre's outfitter's.

No. 148 was originally an ironmonger's belonging to Henry Norrington in the 1840s and 1850s, after which a succession of ironmongers ran the business until it became a tailor's shop in the early 1900s when George Goodacre extended his outfitter's business from next door at No. 147 (and later into No. 149). At No. 149, Joseph Sharp had opened a grocer's shop around 1850 and it remained as such under Richard E. Page through the 1850s to the 1890s. Then George Goodacre moved in during the early 1900s. Through the 1920s and 1930s Nos. 147 to 149 became the London Drapery Stores until John Blundell moved in around 1939. Blundell's were then in occupation into the 1970s.

The *Albion Hotel* at No. 150 stood on the corner of Coleman Street from the 1850s, with Thomas Wolferston as landlord and the Long family in charge from the 1880s until the 1920s. Originally joined to Lankester's Albion Brewery, which stood behind in Coleman Street, it was owned by Forder's Hampton Court Brewery until taken over by Brickwoods in 1925, then finally Whitbread by the time of its closure in 1974. The site was later taken over by the technical college.

Nos. 151 to 153 were once known as Coleman Place, being a terrace of grand houses, of which only No. 153 survives, the others being demolished in the 1960s. No. 151 was home to a variety of residents, including boot maker John Brooks in the 1880s, wardrobe dealer Harry Filsell in the early 1900s and Martin's picture-frame makers in the 1920s and 1930s. No. 152 was home to railway clerk Charles Chandler in the 1840s and 1850s and appears to have been inhabited by employees of the South Western Railway Company though to the 1870s, when Stephen Scott lived there. Scott was manager of the Albion Brewery around the corner in Colman Street. In the 1880s, No. 152 became the Coffee Tavern run by Benjamin Smith, but that venture had gone by 1887 when the Southampton Co-operative Society had moved in.

From the early 1900s it was the residence of surgeon John Tiley Montgomery McDougall, who was successor to the former workhouse surgeon Henry Bencraft, who was listed as being in No. 153 during his association with the workhouse. McDougall was, in turn, succeeded by surgeons Frederick Bacon and Albert Sandy in the 1920s and 1930s when the address became the practice of Berendt, Chambers & Lockhart, which continued until the 1960s.

ST MARY STREET – LOWER EAST SIDE – WORKHOUSE

No. 153 had a long association with the adjacent workhouse, being the home of its medical officer. One of the earliest surgeons was Henry Dusautoy, who lived there in the 1840s and 1850s until Henry Bencraft succeeded him. His son, Henry William Russell Bencraft, was born there in 1858 and, after taking up the profession, became the workhouse medical officer from 1885. Henry Bencraft junior went on to become one of Southampton's most notable citizens with a career in business, sport and politics. The address seems to have disappeared from the directories in the 1880s, possibly

No. 153 was at one time the home of the Workhouse Medical Officer. The building still exists and now forms part of the City College that took over the workhouse after the Second World War.

The rear of No. 153 St Mary Street in its dilapidated, post-war state. After refurbishment it became part of the city college that took over the workhouse buildings after the Second World War. The café at No. 44 can be seen on the left, across the street.

being incorporated as part of the workhouse, and from that date the medical officers associated with the institution are shown as being at No. 152.

The St Mary's Workhouse (officially No. 154) dated from 1776 with a capacity of 220 but became so overcrowded and unsanitary with inmates sleeping four to a bed and

A plan of the workhouse as built in 1868.

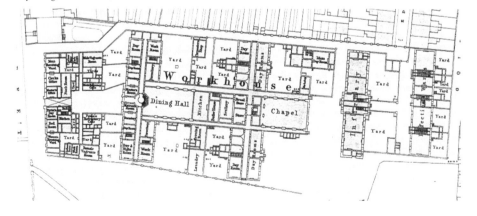

The final assembly of the 'workhouse guardians' in 1930 when the system was abolished. The buildings themselves were later converted to become the town's technical college.

no segregation of men, women and children. A new building was commissioned in 1866 and completed in 1868 when Joseph Bull & Sons were charged with its construction. When completed, it cost 50 per cent over budget at £31,200 through alterations and additions. Its government was, through the 'workhouse guardians', selected parish officials, who oversaw its administration and welfare of the inmates, but the workhouse

The entrance of the former St Mary's Workhouse which now houses the Southampton's City College (Dave Marden).

system was abolished in 1930 and the guardians disbanded. After World War Two, the buildings were taken over and converted into the town's technical college and is now the city college. Immediately to the south of the workhouse, St Mary's Church had stood for centuries and its history is detailed in the final chapter.

ST MARY STREET – SOUTH SIDE – FORMER CHANTRY LAND

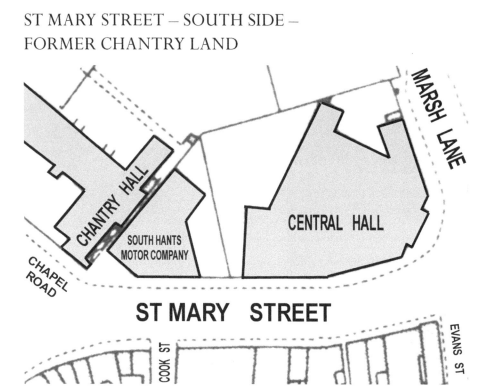

The southern end of St Mary Street where the gardens of the Chantry were replaced by buildings from the 1920s.

Until the 1920s there was nothing along this section of the street apart from the high stone wall that enclosed the gardens of the former Chantry. A section remains along Marsh Lane but the rest came down with the building of the Central Hall, which was completed in 1925 as a Wesleyan church at a cost of £41,000. Quite apart from religious services, the hall has been used as a cinema and a conference hall, most notably when evangelist Billy Graham spoke there in 1954. Despite its multiple uses, the hall fell out of favour and was sold to Hampshire County Council in 1965 as an annex to the city college. It was later purchased by the New Community in 1989 and has since provided

The construction of the Central Hall inside the boundary wall of the former Chantry gardens.

many community events since then.

The newly completed Central Hall. These days it is partially hidden by the Kingsway dual carriageway.

A large crowd gathered for the opening of the Central Hall in 1925. Marsh Lane is the street to the right of the picture.

At around the same time as the Central Hall, the Chantry Hall was built nearby on the corner of Chapel Road and served as a meeting place and community centre, but after several years of declining use it was destroyed by a serious fire in 2007 and the

The South Hants Motor Company staff in the 1950s (Dave Goddard Collection).

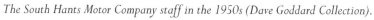

site has been redeveloped for housing. The South Hants Motor Company, who were the main dealers for Ford vehicles, had built their workshops and showrooms between the two halls by the 1930s. It had then become a petrol service station and was occupied by a haulage firm by the 1970s.

ST MARY'S CHURCH

Perhaps the most important building in St Mary Street is the City's mother church, which has a long and interesting history, having existed in some form or other since Saxon times in the settlement of Hamwic during the 700s. In medieval times it was reputedly rebuilt in the 1100s, but by the mid-1500s was in ruin. Over the next couple of centuries several parts were repaired until another complete rebuild occurred between 1878 and 1884 when the church became much of what we see today.

However, at that time it did not have its spire but this was added later, with construction beginning in 1912 and being completed by 5 January 1914. The church's eight bells were installed in May 1914. Having arrived at the Docks (Terminus) station, they were hauled to the church on horse-drawn carts in grand procession.

St Mary's Church as it was before 1878 with its substantial gravestones, tombs and iron railings.

The church as rebuilt in 1884 but without its spire, which wasn't begun until 1912 and completed in 1914.

St Mary's Church in the early 1900s before it gained its spire and, with railings intact (Dave Marden Collection).

The spire under construction and almost complete in 1914.

The bells arrived at the church on 1 May 1914.

During World War Two much of the building was destroyed by bombing, but the bells and tower had been restored by 1948. The remainder of the church was eventually rebuilt between 1954 and 1956. After the rebuilding, one of the more questionable

Services were held in the exposed interior of the church after much of it was destroyed by bombing in 1940.

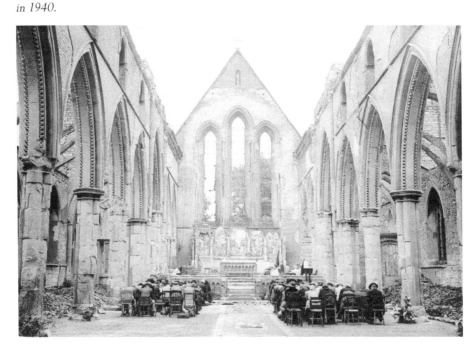

An aerial view of the rebuilding under way in the mid-1950s, which was completed in 1956.

actions was the subsequent removal of the grave headstones, which were broken up and used as low walls along the churchyard paths. The graves themselves are still occupied but are now grassed over and some of those to the north of the church have since been used as a car park.

ND - #0211 - 270225 - C0 - 234/156/9 - PB - 9781780916132 - Gloss Lamination